The Nineteen Letters
of Ben Uziel

Being a Special Presentation of the Principles of Judaism

Rabbi Samson Raphael Hirsch

גלוי וידוע לפניך שלא לכבודי עשיתי ולא לכבוד
בית אבא אלא לכבודך שלא ירבו מחלקת בישראל

"Before Thee it is revealed and known that not for
my glory or the glory of my father's house have I done
this, but for Thy glory that discord may not increase
in Israel."—MEGILLAH, p. 3.

CONTENTS

TRANSLATOR'S PREFACE.

In giving to the English-reading Jewish
public this English version of the maiden effort
of the late great Frankfort Rabbi, Samson Raphael Hirsch, the "Nineteen Letters of Ben
Uziel," I am strongly conscious that I have performed a difficult task very imperfectly. The
work, though limited in extent, and sketchy
in proportions, is of great importance, both as
regards its own intrinsic value, and its effect
upon the history of Judaism. It was epoch-
making in its time, powerfully influencing
contemporary Jewish thought, and paving the
way for the development of a mighty and imposing school in German Judaism; but its
merits are not shown in their just light by a
mere translation. To properly elucidate the
remarkable and original concept of Judaism
which Samson Raphael Hirsch employed for
the rebuilding of the ancient faith upon modern
lines, in noble spiritual harmony with its traditional foundations, would require an elabo-

rate and detailed commentary or treatise, an
effort for which the translator does not, at this
time, feel prepared, and yet without which the
work is necessarily incomplete. The difficulties, too, of the mere translation have been
very great. The author's German style is
terse, energetic, and laden with thought, but
it is a diction all of his own, complicated, and
involved in parts, condensed to the extreme of
brevity in other parts, and full of special terms
and peculiar writings derived from the author's
particular conceptions in regard to Jewish religious notions, or Hebrew philology.   It can
easily be seen that to render such a style into
clear, intelligible, and idiomatic English, and
yet to preserve, in some measure, the striking
characteristics of the original, was a task of im-
mense difficulty.   I have endeavored to per-
form this task to the best of my ability.   I
have aimed to produce a version which should
reflect, however faintly, the beauties of the
original—its solemn earnestness and fiery eloquence, its thought-profundity and rugged di-
rectness, and yet should not be too alien in form,

nor too far removed from the customary speech and diction of English literary style. In this effort I have sometimes reproduced with literal exactness terms and expressions used by the author, and have again ventured to deviate widely from the original text. Such terms as "The All-One," "Man-Israel," and "Deed-Symbol," I have rendered literally, because, although unfamiliar to English readers, they are essential concepts in the theologico-philosophical system of our author; on the other hand, I have disregarded his peculiar writing of Hebrew words — "Yissroel," "Mitzwauss," "Edauss," "Yaakauw," and his use of the colloquialism "Haschem" for "the Lord," "T'nach" for "the Bible," and have substituted in their stead the forms familiar to us; for while Hirsch had good reasons, in his time, for introducing these peculiar forms, to use them in a modern English work would simply be to introduce an entirely unnecessary element of uncouthness and *bizarrerie*. I have also taken the liberty to add words and phrases, and to divide involved and complicated sen-

tences whenever I thought such action necessary to add to the perspicuity and intelligibil-
ity of the rendering.

I now commend my work, which, imperfect
though I feel that it is, has, nevertheless, occupied most of my leisure hours during the past
three years, to the judgment of the English-
reading public interested in the thinkers of
Israel, and the thoughts they think.   If this
version succeeds in drawing the attention of
some to the life-work of one of the noblest
laborers in the vineyard of Israel, " Dreamers
of the Ghetto," called by shallow, carping
lips; if it cause them to ponder a little upon
the meaning of Judaism and its message to the
world, my reward will be as great as I have
dared to hope.

BERNARD DRACHMAN.

New York, Elul, 5658.
September, 1898.

SAMSON RAPHAEL HIRSCH.

A BIOGRAPHICAL SKETCH.

Samson Raphael Hirsch was, indeed, a "prince and a great man" in Israel; a rare and noble figure in the Judaism of the century now so rapidly nearing its end. Our age, so barren of men of original and profound philosophic and religious concepts, of deep convictions and burning enthusiasm; so over-fruitful of weak and inane sciolists, who, parrot-like, repeat the semi - comprehended phrases of pseudo-religious materialism, because through them lies the road to place and pelf, and the approval of the rich and worldly; our age, that could so ill afford it, lost in him one who almost alone towered above the dead level of indifference and mediocrity, and waved on high the banner of Jewish science, Jewish loyalty, and Jewish idealism. Ten years have rolled into the abyss of the past since he took leave of earth; but to those who enjoyed the

inestimable privilege of knowing him, or of
entering into spiritual or intellectual commu-
nion with him, his loss is as fresh, and the pain
as keen, as though but yesterday had witnessed
his demise, for the impression which he produced upon his vast circle of congregants and
admirers was so profound, and the sentiments
of admiration and esteem which he aroused
were so sincere and ardent, that death alone
could suffice to obliterate them. Samson
Raphael Hirsch had also many opponents
during his lifetime, and the aims and objects
for which he toiled and fought with all the
power of his restless brain and his fiery
tongue, were, and still are, subjected to severe
criticism; but in one point all, enemies and
friends, agree, that his life was altogether
great, that his view of Judaism was sublime
in its intellectual grandeur and ethical purity,
and that the manner in which he sought to
realize it was altogether admirable, and
adapted to confer glory and honor upon
Israel in the eyes of the world. Nor did he
live in vain or toil for naught. His life bears

the characteristic indication of the truly great,
that it has been fertile in enduring results; he
was not, like many so-called leaders, merely
an eminent representative of principles, not
actually upheld by those theoretically his adherents, a general without an army; on the
contrary, he possessed the faculty of thoroughly convincing and winning his followers,
of inspiring them with the same enthusiasm
which burnt within his breast.   The future of
Judaism, of the ages-old historical Judaism, is
safe in Germany in the keeping of those reared
under the influence of his spirit, for he gave
them that which alone can secure the well-
being of a religion, profound attachment to it
as the one priceless treasure of their lives, and
an unyielding consistency and fidelity which
will render permanently impossible anything
like profane or sacrilegious trifling with the
precepts of their most sacred heritage.

Nor is the influence of his spirit confined to
the immediate circle of his own congregation,
splendid though this latter be; far beyond the
confines of the queenly city of Frankfort-on-

the-Main, where his chief life-work was done,
throughout Germany, Austro-Hungary, and
Russia, it has worked wonders upon the minds
of Judah's children; and wherever Judaism is
threatened, apparently in its very existence,
and seems hopelessly delivered over to the
twin destructive and disintegrating influences
of modern anti-religionism and mediæval
superstition and unculture, an approach to
the ideal set by Hirsch seems the only way out
of the almost insuperable difficulty.

Samson Raphael Hirsch was born on the
24th of Sivan, 5568 (1808), in the city of
Hamburg, then, as now, an exemplary Jewish
community, renowned for the great number of
its pious and benevolent men and women.
His father was a pious and learned Israelite,
who, though a merchant, devoted much of his
time to Hebrew studies; his grandfather was
Rabbi Mendel Frankfurter, who founded the
Talmud Torah in Hamburg, and was Assistant
Rabbi of the neighboring congregation of
Altona, for which service he never accepted
any compensation. A grand uncle of his

was Rabbi Loeb Frankfurter, the author of the
two Talmudic works, הרכסים לבקעה [1] and
קול יהודה [2], well known in Rabbinical circles.
The power of domestic precept and example
in shaping the religious disposition of the
boy was no doubt great, but there was soon
added to it an influence far more potent in at-
tuning his soul to piety and to that enthusiastic faith in God and Judaism, which never
left him at any period of his life. Isaac
Bernays, of whom Israel's greatest historian,
Graetz, says that he understood the importance of Judaism in the history of the world
far better than Mendelssohn, and that he possessed the ability to inspire his pupils with
joyous devotion to their faith, became, in the
year 1822, Rabbi, or, as he preferred to call himself, following the Portuguese usage, Chacham
of the Hamburg congregation, and under the
influence of his Biblical and Talmudical instruction and earnest sermons the youthful
Hirsch insensibly found himself growing dis-
satisfied with the commercial career for which

---

[1] The Ridges Levelled.   [2] The Voice of Judah.

his parents had designed him, which dissatis-
faction finally culminated in the definite resolve to choose the Rabbinical vocation as his
life task.   In furtherance of this plan he went
to Mannheim, where, under the instruction of
the venerable Rabbi Jacob Ettlinger, after-
ward Rabbi of Altona, he devoted himself as-
siduously to Talmudical studies until 1829,
when he entered the University of Bonn.
Here he came into close connection with a number of Jewish students, whose minds were full
of restless and skeptical thought, and pulsat-
ing with strong ambition for careers of power
and distinction, then, as now, so tremen-
dously difficult for Jews to attain in Germany.
They organized a debating society, and among
the keenest and most brilliant debaters on all
subjects, especially religious, was Samson
Raphael Hirsch.

Abraham Geiger was one of those students,
and a warm personal friend and admirer of
Hirsch, of whose splendid intellectual gifts,
remarkable eloquence, strict moral principles and personal amiability, he draws,

In his posthumous writings, a most attractive picture. Strange, indeed, that two warm friends, issuing from very similar family environments, both sincere and both inspired by genuine desire to work for the welfare of their people and their faith, should have sought the realization of their ideals upon roads so utterly divergent, leading to goals diametrically opposed.

Passing strange, but still a phenomenon which repeats itself in every country and every age, and which we can, without difficulty, see in our own surroundings and time.

Hirsch had hardly passed a year at the University when he was called, in 1830, as Land Rabbi to the Principality of Oldenburg. In Bonn he had been brought face to face with the Jewish religious problem as it manifested itself among the intellectual classes. In Oldenburg he beheld it in all its difficulty and apparent insolubility among the middle and lower classes, the mercantile and laboring elements of the Jewish people. These twain experiences were undoubtedly hard blows to

his ideal, but, instead of discouraging him,
they aroused his latent energy, and strength-
ened in him the resolve to do his utmost to
secure the wide dissemination and propagation
of the true meaning of Judaism, as he understood it, and which through hard study and
profound reflection had already at that youthful period ripened in him to a firm and solemn
conviction.   The first fruit of this resolve was
one of the most, if not the most, significant
and characteristic of his productions, the
epoch-making writing entitled " Neunzehn
Briefe über Judenthum, von Ben Uziel,"
which appeared in Altona in 1836, and which
is the subject of the present translation.   The
fact that he published it under a pseudonym
is characteristic for his intensity and single-
ness of purpose.   Youth usually delights in
publicity, and loves to concentrate the attention of the world upon itself, but he had no
such object in view.   He did not seek for
fame, neither should his name, although his
official position must have lent it some weight,
assist in procuring a favorable reception for

his book. Not the name or position of the
author, but what he had to say should attract
attention, should give his co-religionists food
for thought. But the fact of his authorship
did not remain long unknown; the letters
made a profound impression in German Jewish
circles, and soon all knew that the youthful
Rabbi of Oldenburg was the author of the
eloquent and original defense of Orthodox
Judaism. In the nineteen letters, which
assume to be the correspondence between a
young Rabbi called Naphtali (נ״צ=Hirsch),
and his youthful friend Benjamin, who, though
originally religious, had, through contact with
the world and the perusal of non-Jewish writings, lost his early convictions, Hirsch set up
that view of Judaism called in Germany
"Denkgläubigkeit," which we may translate
as "intellectual or enlightened Orthodoxy," although he himself was intolerant of any name
except Judaism or "Torah." The nineteen
letters are a sort of modern *Moreh Nebuchim*,
"Guide of the Perplexed," though very different in form and contents from the famous work

of the Cordovan philosopher, to whose theory of Judaism, its tenets and its law, Hirsch was strongly opposed. Like Maimonides, however, he addressed himself neither to the simple-minded believer, who found in the observance of his ancestral faith sufficiency of strength and solace for the battle of life, and nourishment for his intellectual and spiritual cravings, nor to the religious Nihilist to whom the whole of theology is but an exploded standpoint, but to the "perplexed," to those whose hearts still clung with warmest attachment to Judaism, but whose minds found much doubtful, incomprehensible, or seemingly purposeless in the faith endeared to them by a thousand ties.

In classic German, with a style ofttimes highly poetic and eloquent, and always impressive, and with masterly argumentation, he proceeded to confute their objections. Commencing with the demonstration of the necessity of the existence of God, as a *conditio sine qua non* of the universe, he follows with the postulate of the need of a human race to carry into actuality the infinite potentiality of good in the Deity. But with freedom of the will comes the inevitable conflict between good and evil; humanity will not devote itself as a whole to the maintenance of the Divine law, the free will left to itself would soon produce an utter confusion of notions concerning good and evil. Hence the need of an entire community which shall dedicate itself entirely to the mission of teaching humanity to seek for the good, or what is the same, to obey the will of God. Such a people must have distinctive laws and customs to sanctify it and distinguish it from the mass of external humanity as especially consecrated to the service of God. This duty has been historically assumed by Israel; these distinctive laws form the ceremonial legislation of the Torah. Then follows the analysis of the Torah and the demonstration that every part is essential and necessary, either to the furtherance of the ideal of good on the part of mankind, or the establishment of Israel in its character of " servant of the All-One," and that no human

authority has power to abrogate any of the
Divine institutions. Hirsch's system of what
he calls the "scientific upbuilding of Judaism" (wissenschaftlicher Aufbau des Judenthum's) is somewhat peculiar. While he
insists that the doctrinal and ethical contents
of Judaism can only be ascertained by absolute objectivity of investigation into its Biblical and Talmudic sources, uninfluenced by
prejudices or notions drawn from extraneous
spheres of thought, he utterly refuses to consider the question of the authenticity of revelation and the binding character of Jewish
codes. For him the Torah is axiomatic, as
unquestionably real as nature itself. To
doubt or question this would be to put oneself
outside of Judaism. While the first principle
is truly scientific and must, of necessity, be
approved by all, the second principle can not
but be a serious difficulty to many an honest
mind. Nor can it be denied that in the practical application of the first principle, the
objective investigation of the Torah, he was
occasionally guilty of both philosophical and

philological extravagances, which were sharply
and deservedly attacked by his opponents.
Nevertheless, as a whole, his work is profound and acute, and will have enduring
value.

The publication of this work marked an
epoch in the history of Judaism in Germany,
and, indeed, in the world. It showed that
orthodox Judaism was not maintained solely
by the superstitious, or narrow-minded older
generation, who had never been initiated into
the science and culture of the age; but that it
could be warmly, nay, enthusiastically, upheld
by one who had thoroughly acquainted himself with the most daring researches of the new
time, and met them with equally bold and open
argument. More on this account, even, than because of the convincingness of the general theory, or the brilliancy of the special argument,
the letters made a sensation, and aroused universal admiration. The lofty idealism which pervaded his description of the Israel-mission, the
emphasis with which he pointed it out as particularly the duty of the cultured and wealthy

to remain attached with entire and unswerv-
ing faithfulness to the religion and the people
charged with so sublime a task, were admirably
adapted to reach the hearts of the impression-
able and earnest-thinking in Israel. A sensual
or worldly-minded person found nothing attractive in the man or his ideas, but those
possessed of higher impulses, and who seri-
ously pondered over the problem of life and
sought for light and truth, were at once
won over by his profundity and evident sin-
cerity, and among this best class of Israel he
gained numerous and devoted followers. It
was during his tenure of the Rabbinical office
at Oldenburg that he received an unusually
gifted and talented student, whose name was
also destined to shine resplendent in the Jewish world. On the 8th of May, 1837, Hein-
rich Hirsch Graetz, destined to be known as
the father of Jewish history, then in his twen-
tieth year, became the disciple of the already
renowned Oldenburg Rabbi. The impression
produced upon the brilliant and earnest young
thinker by his new teacher is well described in

the memoir of Professor Graetz by Rabbi Dr.
Philipp Bloch, recently published under the
auspices of the Jewish Publication Society,[1]
and this description gives us an excellent
characterization of the personality of Hirsch:
"In Samson Raphael Hirsch he met a man
whose spiritual elevation and noble character
compelled his profound reverence, and who
fully realized all the expectations he had har-
bored concerning him.   Hirsch was a man of
modern culture, and his manner was distinguished, even aristocratic, although he kept
aloof from all social intercourse. He was short
of stature, yet those who came in contact with
him were strongly impressed by his external
appearance, on account of his grave, dignified
demeanor, forbidding familiarity. With great
intellectual gifts, and rare qualities of the
heart, he combined varied theological attain-
ments, and an excellent classical education.
. . . He was the only teacher from whom
Graetz's self-centred being received scientific

---

[1] Index volume of Graetz's "History of the Jews." Philadel-
phia. 1898.

stimulation; perhaps the only man to exercise, so far as the stubborn peculiarity of Graetz's nature permitted it, permanent influence upon his reserved, independent nature.''

In 1838 Hirsch published, as a necessary concomitant of the letters, his '' Choreb—Essays on Yissroel's Duties in the Dispersion,''[1] which is a text-book on Judaism for the educated youth of Israel. Each law, ceremonial, ethical, or devotional, is thoroughly explained according to the part which it takes in the vast edifice of the ordinances designed to protect Israel in its devotion to the God-idea, or to assist in the diffusion of Jewish spiritual and ethical truth. In 1839 he published '' First Communications from Naphtali's Correspondence.''[2] This was a polemical essay against the reforms of Holdheim and others, and in it he showed himself a master of controversy. With incontrovertible reasoning and biting satire he exposed the utter hollowness and unworthiness of the so-called '' Jewish re-

---

[1] Versuche über Jissroel's Pflichten in der Zerstreuung.
[2] Erste Mittheilungen aus Naphtali's Briefwechsel.

forms," as compared with the old, unadulter-
ated Judaism, and that the latter alone could
enable Israel to fulfill its mission.   In 1841 he
was elected Land-Rabbi of the Hanoverian
districts of Aurich and Osnabrück, with his
residence in Emden.

In 1844 appeared "Second Communications from a Correspondence Concerning the
most Recent Jewish Literature," [1] which contained a vigorous polemic against the contemporary reform movement in Judaism.   In 1846
he received the highest compliment which
could be paid to an orthodox Rabbi by being
called to the Rabbinate of Nicolsburg in Moravia, which such distinguished Talmudists and
representatives of the old school as Rabbi Mor-
dechai Baneth and Rabbi Nahum Trebitsch
had held.   That such a community should
have at that period selected a man of modern
culture as their spiritual head, without any
suspicion of the genuineness of his piety, was,
in itself, exceptional, and a high honor; but it

[1] Zweite Mittheilungen aus einem Briefwechsel über die neueste jüdische Literatur.

was succeeded the next year by a still greater
distinction, when he was installed as Land-
Rabbi of Moravia and Austrian Silesia. This
showed the high repute in which both his
learning and piety stood in communities of un-
questioned orthodoxy. In Austria he passed
five busy and useful years in the reorganization
of the Jewish congregations, the instruction
of numerous disciples, and also, at one time in
public politics, as a member of the Moravian
Parliament. In 1851 he did the most heroic
deed of his life; a deed which demonstrated
most unmistakably that Judaism and truth
only, not worldly glory or reward, were his
life's single purpose. At that time Frankfort-
on-the-Main was, as regards its Jewish congregation, entirely in the hands of the reformers.
Frankfort, ranking with Worms as the oldest
of South German communities, where our ancestors had, during the dark mædieval days,
shown such patient endurance and active hero-
ism in the cause of the sacred faith, was now
given over to the reign of superficial and irrev-
erent innovators. Eleven sincerely pious men

only had withdrawn from the general community and founded the organization which they
did not even venture to call a congregation,
but modestly styled a society, "Israelitische
Religions Gesellschaft."[1] These eleven timidly and hesitatingly sent a request to the Chief
Rabbi of Moravia and Silesia to be their guide
and adviser, hoping that his well-known Jewish enthusiasm, and his financial position,
which permitted him to be independent, would,
perhaps, induce him to accept their call. And
he accepted it. The recognized head of Judaism in two great provinces, clothed with state
authority, loved and honored by his congregations, laid down his brilliant and lucrative
position in order to accept a questionable place
as Rabbi of a small group in a great city, where
the Jewish community at large was thoroughly
organized under other, and hostile, leadership. It was a wise and far-seeing step. Hirsch
recognized that here in the heart of Germany
was the spot where the best and most substan-
tial work could be done for Judaism, for, if he

[1] Israelitish Society for Religion.

could materially elevate the cause of conservatism in Germany, it would inevitably be productive of the most beneficial results in all those neighboring regions which look up to Germany as the model of culture and enlightenment.

His work in Germany was blessed to a degree far beyond what he could have anticipated.

Little by little, through hard, unceasing toil and struggle, he succeeded in developing new Jewish life, and in organizing a model orthodox congregation, numbering some five hundred of the best Jewish families of the place, and provided with all necessary institutions in the most splendid manner. Nor did he confine his efforts to the synagogue; he succeeded in organizing two schools, "Bürgerschule" and "Realschule," in which a thorough Jewish training goes hand in hand with the secular education demanded by the age, thereby securing the youth and thoroughly preparing them to take the place in the congregation occupied by their parents. As conscientious and careful teacher, as eloquent and brilliant preacher, he labored for the advancement of his own congregation, as learned and instructive writer for Judaism in general. As writer his efforts were distributed between contributions to the columns of the "Jeshurun," established in 1854, and independent works. In the twelve years from 1866 to 1878 he published his masterly "Translation of the Pentateuch with Commentary."[1] The leading principle of this great work is to prove the historical unity of Judaism, that it can not be divided into different forms and distinct periods of development, but that its latest manifestations are the logical and necessary postulates of Biblical revelation. During all these years he was battling for liberty of conscience to secure the abrogation of the law, designed in the interests of order and system, but iniquitous in its undesigned consequences, compelling Israelites to remain contributing members of the local congregations, even when these latter had departed from the standards of religious duty. These efforts were finally crowned with success

---

[1] Uebersetzung und Erklärung des Pentatench.

when the bill introduced by Lasker in the German Parliament, permitting Israelites to sever their connection with the congregation without leaving Judaism, became a law on the 28th of July, 1876. Hirsch was forced to this step by the unreasonable actions of the reform Jewish communal authorities of Frankfort, who refused his congregation absolutely necessary privileges, even after it had swelled to hundreds of families. On this subject he wrote two essays, "The Principle of Religious Liberty," [1] 1874, and "On Leaving the Congregation," [2] 1876.

He did not find universal approval of this step, however, even among the orthodox. His most notable opponent was Rabbi S. B. Bamberger, of Würzburg, with whom he had a warm controversy, and a large section of the orthodox Jews under leadership of Dr. Hurwitz remained in connection with the main body of the Frankfort community. In 1882 appeared his "Translation and Explana-

---

[1] Das Princip der Gewissensfreiheit.
[2] Der Austritt aus der Gemeinde.

tion of the Psalms."[1] This work is carried
out in accordance with his established views,
and is distinguished by elegance of rendering,
a painstaking attempt to penetrate the innermost meaning of each psalm, and a scrupulous
adherence to the received text. His effort to
find symbolical meanings in the enigmatical
superscriptions can not, however, be considered
particularly successful. In 1884 he published
an essay "On the relations of the Talmud to
Judaism,"[2] to defend the Talmudic literature
against the vile slanders which anti-Semitic
writers were then already beginning to circu-
late. After this he did but little, the state of
his health precluding active literary or minis-
terial work. He left, however, in manuscript
a translation and explanation of the prayer-
book, which has since been published. In
this connection it is interesting to note, as an
illustration of the high repute in which he
stood among the vast body of his co-religionists in the Russian empire, that shortly after

---

[1] Uebersetzung und Erklärung der Psalmen.
[2] Ueber die Beziehungen des Talmuds zum Judenthum.

his death a translation of the "Nineteen Letters" into classic Hebrew by M. S. Aronsohn appeared in Wilna, and within a few months several editions were exhausted. He died with the dying year, quietly and painlessly, December 31, 1888. Such was the life and such the work of one who was undoubtedly one of the most remarkable figures in Israel's gallery of great men during the present century. Like all great men he had his faults. He was an extremist, but only extremists achieve success. The undecided and weak-kneed compromisers can never control, but are always controlled by their surroundings; but he was a master-mind who led his contemporaries, and his was a powerful and unyielding will, which stamped upon his time the impress of his ideas and convictions. The secret of his success lay, in addition to his own personality, in the absolute consistency of his religious system. His doctrine of consistent obedience to the will of God and the ceremonial law, as a part of that will, in order thereby to accomplish the mission of Israel, was convincing to the minds of thousands, and inspired them with enthusiasm and devotion.

He covered orthodox Judaism with glory by demonstrating that the old synagogue ritual, so bitterly attacked and decried, not only best expressed the true spirit of Judaism, but could be carried out in a highly dignified, impressive, and æsthetic manner.   He has been accused by advocates of the so-called Radical Judaism of making the synagogue service an antiquarian show.   This accusation is, however, utterly superficial.   Whatever of the antique his synagogue service presented was due, not to his inception, but to the laws which, as a true Israelite, he was bound to hold sacred and to obey.   The service in radical temples is undoubtedly not at all antiquarian.   It is modern, but because it is a purely modern conventional arrangement, with very much of the nineteenth century in it, but very little of Judaism and its sacred heritage of inviolable law.   The credit of having boldly taken his standpoint within, not without, Judaism, and having elevated and glorified it by demonstrating its intrinsic beauty and merit, and its own native adequacy for every spiritual want of humanity, will forever belong to Samson Raphael Hirsch, and his name will live imperishable in the history of Israel as one who was in every fiber of his being a Jew, an idealist, and a true friend of mankind.

THE TRANSLATOR.

AUTHOR'S PREFACE.

These letters came into my hands as the legacy of a dear friend. Much of their contents attracted me greatly, and altogether they appeared to me to consider many subjects of high importance from such new and unusual points of view, that I hope by placing them before my brethren to earn their thanks, even if all of the sentiments therein expressed should not meet with universal approval.

The essays alluded to in the last letter are also extant; and I desire the publication of these letters to be considered as a sort of question to the public, whether I should also publish those essays. The voices which will be heard in regard to these letters will also determine me in reference to those writings.

Should the essays appear, then these letters will take the place of the introductory outlines with which, according to the nineteenth letter, the author had intended to preface his book.

As for the letters themselves, I give them just
as I found them, and have not even taken the
liberty, considering that they are the work of
another, to improve here and there occasional
awkwardnesses of style, fearing that I might
perhaps at the same time obliterate some
essential peculiarity.   Out of a subsequently
found later letter of Naphtali to Benjamin,
who appears to have communicated to him
the judgment of a friend concerning this correspondence, I think it not improper to quote
here the following passage :

" Do not forget, my dear Benjamin, that I
did not attempt in the sketches to map out for
you an accurate design of the entire ground-
plan and superstructure, but only a general
outline of the edifice of Judaism.   I have only
led you through one majestic nave of the
edifice, from which you can form a partial
conception of the imposing whole.   I desired
to familiarize your mind and heart at first
only with one chief idea of Judaism, one
which should lead us most speedily to the
sought-for goal, and could not therefore con·

sider all that which your friend otherwise would be right in missing.''

To this I would only add the request to reserve one's judgment concerning special points in these letters until one has read them completely, and pursued further the superficially suggested ideas. I, at least, while at first not a little amazed at many statements, learned subsequently to think quite differently concerning them; much, especially of the contents of the thirteenth and fourteenth letter, I could only comprehend after I had seen the essays.

Finally, I would express the wish that I may not be deceived in the opinion that this correspondence may contain the impulse to much good, and that through the judgment of able and sagacious men I may feel myself encouraged also to publish the essays.

THE AUTHOR.

THE NINETEEN LETTERS OF BEN UZIEL

FIRST LETTER.

MY DEAR NAPHTALI:

When, recently, on the occasion of your trip through the town of my residence, we were privileged to meet again, after many years of separation, for a short fleeting hour, you did not imagine, my dear Naphtali, what interest the subject of our conversation had— and, indeed, still has—for me. You found me so changed in my religious views and practices that, despite your habitual tolerance, you could not suppress the questions which rose, as it were, spontaneously to your lips, "Since when?" and "Why?" As answer I gave you a whole series of accusations against Judaism, concerning which my eyes had been

opened by reading and contact with the world
since I had left home and parents.

You listened quietly to my speech, and,
when I had done, replied, "Do you believe
that you really understand the object which
you are thus condemning?   Have you acquired with your own eyes, and by dint of
honest, earnest investigation, an actual understanding of a matter which, inasmuch as it is
the holiest and most important consideration
of our life, should at least not be cast aside
thoughtlessly and unreflectingly?"   You
showed me that the only sources of my knowledge were, on the one hand, the mechanical
practice of parental customs and a few imperfect and undigested fragments of the Bible and
Talmud acquired from Polish teachers, and, on
the other hand, Christian writers, modern reformers, and especially that view of life which
our present age has brought forth, and which
has, as its chief endeavor, the suppression of
the inner voice of conscience in favor of the
external demands of comfort and ease.

I was forced to confess the insufficiency of my

knowledge, begged you for instruction; then the coachman called, and, in bidding me good-by, you had only time to call " in writing." You have, therefore, made me distrustful, my dear Naphtali, of the opinions I have hitherto held, but you have not refuted them, nor given me better ones in their stead. I, therefore, take advantage of your kind permission, and repeat to you in writing a number of my charges, not for the purpose of defending my present mode of life, but in the sincere desire of information and guidance. Every religion, I believe, should bring man nearer to his ultimate end. This end, what else can it be than the attainment of happiness and perfection?

But if we take these principles as a criterion for Judaism, what utterly depressing results do we not obtain? To what happiness does Judaism conduct its professors? From time immemorial misery and slavery have been their lot; misunderstood or despised by the other nations, and while the rest of mankind mounted to the summit of culture, prosperity, and fortune, its adherents remained always poor in everything which makes human beings great and noble, and which beautifies and dignifies existence.

The Law itself interdicts all enjoyments, is a hindrance to all the pleasures of life. For two thousand years we are as the plaything of fate, as a ball tossed from hand to hand, even in the present time driven from all the paths of happiness. And as for the perfecting of human acquirements, what culture, what conquests in the domain of science, art, or invention, in a word, what great achievements have Jews wrought compared with Egyptians, Phœnicians, Greeks, Romans, Italians, French, English, or Germans?

Robbed of all the characteristics of nationality, we are, nevertheless, deemed a nation, and every one of us is by his very birth doomed to form an additional link in this never-ending chain of misery. The Law is chiefly at fault for all this: by enjoining isolation in life, and thereby arousing suspicion and hostility; by breaking the spirit through the inculcation of humble submissiveness, thereby inviting contempt; by discouraging the pursuit of the formative arts; by dogmas which bar the way of free speculation, and by removing, through the separation in life, every incentive to exertion in science and art, which, therefore, do not flourish among us.

As for our own lore, it perverts the mind and leads it astray into subtleties and the *minutiæ* of petty distinctions, until it becomes incapable of entertaining simple and natural opinions, so that I have always wondered not a little how you, who have taste and understanding for the beauties of Virgil, Tasso, and Shakespeare, and who are able to penetrate into the consistent structures of Leibnitz or Kant, can find pleasure in the rude and tasteless writings of the Old Testament, or in the illogical disputations of the Talmud?

And what effect has it, the Law, upon heart and life? The broad principles of universal morality are narrowed into anxious scrupulosity about insignificant trifles; nothing is taught except to fear God, everything, even the pettiest details of life, is referred directly

to God; life itself becomes a continuous mon-
astic service, nothing but prayers and ceremonies; he the most praiseworthy Jew, who
lives most secluded, and knows least of the
world, though he permits it to support him, but
wastes his life in fasting and praying, and the
perusal of senseless writings. Look yourself
at the book which is put into our hands as the
"Path of Life," [1] and which contains the
whole duty of the Jew, what else does it teach
except praying and fasting and the keeping
of holidays? Where is there one word of the
active, busy life around us? And this, too,
just in our time? Why, it is quite impossible
to keep these laws intended for an entirely
different time. What limitation in travelling,
what embarrassment in association with Gentiles, what difficulties in every business !

   Please, please do not point, for an answer,
to the reformistic tendencies of the age, how
little by little everything is being cut away
which does not harmonize with the conception
of the destiny of man or the needs of the

---

[1] אורח חיים—

time. Is not this in itself a step outside of Judaism ?

Should one not rather, if one is a Jew, consistently carry out these notions, instead of attaching oneself to such contradictory principles, by which nothing can be attained except capricious, fortuitous patchwork ?

And, besides, for this very reform, everything is lacking, unity, legally constituted legislative bodies, authority. All of these efforts are only the doings of individuals, the most divergent opinions prevail among the Rabbis and preachers; while some as enlightened men of the time tear down, others hold fast to the rotten building, and wish themselves to be buried under it. I myself recently saw a young Rabbi who, whenever he travels, in simple-minded piety, contents himself with prisoner's fare, and whom, when one visits him, one may still find poring over the folios of the Talmud; nay, he is even said to grieve earnestly over the fact that some of the members of his congregation are so far advanced in enlightenment that they do not close their places of business on the Sabbath. What shall become of us, dear Naphtali? I am about to marry, but, God knows, when I think that perhaps I shall be called upon to exercise the duties of a father to children, I tremble.

Excuse me, dear friend, that I have spoken so freely and unreservedly, although I know that you revere all this very much, and, I suppose, must do so as Rabbi, on account of your position; still I am confident that you have so much love left for me from former days, that you will, in answering me, forget your office; for what *that* teaches, I know sufficiently well. Farewell.   Your

BENJAMIN.

SECOND LETTER.

Because I answer you so soon, dear Benjamin, do not think I have not maturely reflected upon the subjects which you put before me in your letter.

You know that in my earliest youth these subjects employed my soul, that, reared by enlightened but God-fearing parents, the voices of T'nach[1] early spoke to my spirit, and that, of my own free will, when my intelligence had already matured, I permitted the T'nach to lead me to Gemara[2]—that not external necessity caused me to select the vocation of Rabbi, but my own inner life-plan. So much the more do I wonder that you can fear to find in me the hypocrisy of office. I would be angry with you, were you not my friend, were I not yours. But that is the curse of the time and the fatal obstacle to beneficent activity on the part of those in official station, that that

---
[1] Bible.　[2] Talmud.

9

which should be the treasured possession of all, has become the attribute of office, so that people are inclined to look upon the universal rule of life as the mere regulation of an order and say, " Yes, *he* must be so, must speak so, his position—his bread—demands it." Sad degradation of the age ! It seems quite natural that a man should sell everything, his most cherished individuality, his inmost convictions, for bread, and everything is deemed excusable if it but yield bread, bread ! But perhaps you rejoice, Benjamin, and thousands with you, that all of this has been forced to flee for refuge within the limits of an official class, for in this you may see a hope—and indeed a prospect—that it will soon be expelled even from there, and the consistent process of erecting life upon the twin foundation principles of happiness and perfection, suspended between heaven and earth, and supported by themselves, may soon begin.

Excuse me this excitement, dear friend; I will also try to forget that you spoke so. I proceed, therefore, to answer your letter, and can dispense, I hope, without fear of angering you, with the giving of a special assurance that my official station will not influence my reply.

You estimate the value of Judaism by the principle of the purpose of human existence, and this, in your view, is found in happiness and perfection. I could ask: Is it so sure that happiness and perfection form the goal and object of man's being? I could ask upon what basis you found this opinion, or what could you answer to the careless pleasure-seeker or criminal, who thinks the excitement and sensual lust of the moment a greater happiness than all temporal or eternal blessings? Every one must be permitted to be his own judge of what constitutes happiness for him, for happiness decreed in accordance with any compulsory external standard, ceases to be happiness! And the perfecting of one's being, the mounting of the highest intellectual heights! By how few ever attained, by how few attainable!

Truth itself is conceived by a thousand

thinkers in a thousand different ways.   To
neglect its pursuit is, after all, only a sin
against oneself, and, therefore, one can only
be accountable to oneself.   For to whom would
I owe an accounting, if this principle only demands the promotion of the happiness and perfection of others as a means of attaining my
own, and I relinquish this?   How, I would ask
you, is it with the multitude of unhappy and
imperfect ones outside of Judaism?   But I will
omit all these questions.   Let us put aside for
a while the standard of measurement, and let
us try to know that which we desire to measure—Judaism, in its history and teachings.
Perhaps, on the way, we may learn to think
differently concerning the destiny of mankind, and may obtain a different mode of dis-
cerning the purpose of the existence of the
nations, and their duties.   But we must become
acquainted with it from the source which it
itself points out to us; which it has rescued
from the wreck of all its other fortunes as the
only original document and source of instruction concerning its true essence—from its To-

rah. Its history we must learn from it, for
Judaism is an historical phenomenon, and for
its origin, its first entrance into history, and
for a long subsequent time, the Torah is the
only monument. And if, at the cradle of this
people, we were to hear mystic voices, such as
no other nation ever heard—voices announc-
ing the purpose of this people's existence—for
which it entered into history, should we not
hearken to these voices, and try to comprehend
them, that we might thus understand it and its
history? It is the only source of its law, written and oral. Therefore, to the Torah! But,
before we open it, let us consider how we shall
read it. Not for the purpose of making philological and antiquarian investigations, nor to
find support and corroboration for antediluvian
or geological hypotheses, nor either in the expectation of unveiling supermundane myste-
ries, but as Jews must we read it—that is to
say, looking upon it as a book given to us by
God that we may learn from it to know ourselves—what we are, and what we should be
in this our earthly existence. It must be to

us *Torah*—that is, instruction and guidance in
this divine world; a generator of spiritual life
within us.   Our desire is to apprehend Judaism; therefore, we must take up our position
in thought within Judaism, and must ask ourselves, "What will human beings be who recognize the contents of this book as a basis and
rule of life given to them by God?"   In the
same way we must seek understanding of the
mitzvoth, the commandments—that is to say,
we must strive to know their extent and bearing from the written and oral law.   All of this
must take place from the standpoint of the
object of all this procedure, the finding of the
true law of life.   Only when you have thus
comprehended Judaism from itself, as it repre-
sents itself to be, and have then found it untenable and unworthy of acceptance, may you, if
you wish, cast upon it the stone of obloquy.
We must also read the Torah *in Hebrew*—that
is to say, in accordance with the spirit of that
language.   It describes but little, but through
the rich significance of its verbal roots it paints
in the word a picture of the thing.

It only joins for us predicate to subject, and sentence to sentence; but it presupposes the listening soul so watchful and attentive that the deeper sense and profounder meaning, which lie not upon but below the surface, may be supplied by the independent action of the mind itself. It is, as it were, a semi-symbolic writing. With wakeful eye and ear, and with soul roused to activity, we must read; nothing is told us of such superficial import that we need only, as it were, accept it with half roused dreaminess; we must strive ourselves to create again the speaker's thoughts, to think them over, or the sense will escape us. We must follow also the same method in studying the *mitzvoth*, when they assign a purpose for any particular object, or ordain some symbolic practice. There we must strive to discover analytically the correction of the purpose with this particular object; here the natural method of practically expressing such an idea in consideration of its reason and connection. I only point out to you the path which I have followed. To you I shall give only direct results, and that only, for the present, in general outlines; later, if you wish, you shall learn the details, and also the reasons for the methods of investigation.

Now, let us read. May you forget all the annoyance which the reading of these writings caused you in your youth; forget all the prejudices which you may have imbibed from different sources against these writings. Let us read as though we had never read them; as though we had never heard of them. Let us arouse in our soul the life questions, "What is the world in me, and around me, to me? What am I; what should I be to it? What am I; what should I be as man-Israel?"

With such interrogative spirit let us read, and receive the answer as Jews, from the mouth of the being who alone can give the explanation—from Deity. Farewell.

THIRD LETTER.

I have left you time till this letter, so that the life-questions which I touched upon toward the end of the previous letter might grow within you, and that you might perhaps have already taken into your hand in the proper frame of mind the book of life. We will now open it together. You will agree, my Benjamin, that what we wish is to become acquainted with Israel, to learn the import and significance of this name, which we bear by reason of birth, what we are and should be as bearers thereof. But Israel is an historical phenomenon among the other manifestations of the world's records, and therefore the next question is, what is the meaning of history? History, however differently we may conceive it, is without doubt the way to fulfill the destiny of man in universal humanity, therefore the next question is, what is man, what should he be? But man is not isolated, he is a creature amidst the other creatures, affected

17.

by and affecting them; therefore we must next
ask, what is the world ?   Israel, history, mankind, the world—they all can only be comprehended through God, the creator, as a work
of art is only then perfectly understood, when
we have an insight into the plans of the
master, and to our eye God reveals himself
only in His works.   Thus the Torah—the
Divine Book of the Law—leads through the
concept of Israel and Israel's duties, to the
knowledge of God, the world, the missions of
mankind, and history.   Let us follow the law
upon this path.

The Torah summons us to view heaven and
earth and speaks " from heaven to earth, from
earth to heaven, everything which thou seest
existing, when it came into existence, בראשית
ברא אלהים in its beginning God was active
as its creator.   Seest thou the heaven in its
eternally silent, unchanging course, bearer of
light and heat and all the motive forces of our
earth, supporter of the earth-world, seest thou
it with its millions of starry worlds, or
resplendent with the refulgence of the magnif-

icently radiant sun-ball, or the earth, the swift runner,[1] with its eternal circles of originating and passing away, of blooming and withering, of life and death, eternally struggling from ceasing, fading, and death, to ever new existence, bloom, and life; dost thou see it with its millions of productions, stones, plants, animals, all of which it produces, nourishes, and again takes back into its bosom; dost thou see the light, the messenger of heaven to earth, which coaxes all to life and leads from life, through which thou seest everything which is, and everything arrays itself for thee in resplendent colors; dost thou see the firmament spread out around the earth, which receives the ray of light, and alters it to suit the necessity of the earth, in which the clouds move and water the parched earth, the thirsty grasses, and beasts, and men? Seest thou the universal ocean, with all-encompassing arm of flood embracing the earth, or the springs which burst forth from the fissures of the rocks and flow on as rivulets, brooks,

---

[1] A play in the term ארץ from רוץ to run.

and mighty rivers? Dost thou rejoice in the firm surface of the earth upon which thou walkest safe and secure together with thy dear ones; hast thou pleasure in its meadowy expanse or its leafy trees, or in all the living beings which stir so animatedly in the waters and in the air, or dwell with thee on earth? Dost thou see sun, moon, and stars, which from their celestial positions above thee regulate the times of day and month and the seasons of the year, and determine the recurring periods of waking and sleep, of rise and fall, of bloom and decay on earth?

" One God exists, one omnipotent Creator," proclaims the Torah; "through His word all which is was created." Heaven and earth are His work; His are light and air, sea and dry land; His, plants and fishes, birds, insects, and all beasts; His, creation sun, moon, and stars. He spake וַיְהִי and it was. Behold now separately each created thing, from the blade of grass to the vast sun-ball, each with its special purpose and each specially adapted in its form and matter for that purpose; the same

Almighty wisdom formed and designated each for its special purpose. This Divine wisdom proclaimed to the light, " serve the day ; " to the darkness, " serve the night ; " to the firmament, " be the heaven over the earth ; " to the gathering of waters, " be thou the ocean ; " to the dry substance, " become earth, scene of life and development ; " to the planets, " be ye rulers of the seasons." It determined the purpose, and according to the purpose, it ordained for its object matter, form, force, and dimensions. It spake, ויהי כן and it was as it is. Infinitesimally small or infinitely great, all was created by the word of God, determined by His will, formed by His finger. All the forces which thou seest working in everything, and all the laws, according to which they work and which thou noticest and admirest; from the force and the law, in obedience to which a stone falls or a seed of corn grows into a plant; to the force and the law in accordance with which the planets move in their orbits or thy intellect expands; to God, the Universal Force, they all belong; His word prevails in every law.

Now, notice again this great throng of beings, tho separated and distinguished by peculiar construction and different purposes, yet united in one great harmonious system, each working in its own place, its own time, and according to its own measure of force, none interfering with the other, each bearing the All and born by the All. Who is it that has harmonized all these opposites and united the countless into the All? ויברל אלהים בין האור ובין החשך. It is the same All-One who has established harmony between light and darkness, between life and death. As His love supplies matter and force to work, so also does the finger of His justice point limitation, goal, and measure. "Harmonizer of Contrasts is His name." And everything which He created, formed, and arranged—ויברך אלהים—He also blessed with the blessing of permanence and development. Not only all *was* through Him, all *is* through Him. His blessing is every bloom and blossom; His blessing every germ and every fruit; His blessing the mother's offspring; His blessing the babe pressed to the loving breast. And He—who created, formed, blessed, and ordered—ויפנש—invisible as the soul in thy body—He withdrew from gaze and concealed, like the soul, in His creation He continues to work, preserve and develop, invisible. His work thou seest, His formations thou admirest, His laws thou searchest out, His blessings thou enjoyest, but Him, the Creator, Shaper, Orderer, Benefactor of the world, Him thy mortal eye shall ne'er behold. Therefore, when thou seest and wonderest, studiest, and enjoyest, bend the knee and adore Him, the Only One, who created and formed, ordered and blessed, and worship Him as power, wisdom, justice, and love universal and eternal.

" Attribute to God all the offspring of forces,
Attribute to God all glory and power!
Attribute to God the revelation of His name,
Bow down to Him in raiment of the sanc-
    tury!
The voice of God is upon the waters,

The Almighty One of creation thunders,
God is upon the mighty floods.
The voice of God is in every force,
The voice of God is inall beauty.
The voice of God breaketh the cedars,
God shattereth the forests of Lebanon,
He causeth them to skip like the foal,
Lebanon and Siryon as the young Re'ëm.
The voice of God splitteth the flaming fire,
The voice of God terrifieth the wilderness,
God affrighteth the wilderness of Kadesh!
The voice of God maketh the gazelles give
    birth,
And strippeth bare the forests.
And in the temple of His worship
His All proclaims ' Revelation.'   (Psalm
    xxix.)''

.   .   .   .

" Even for this doth my heart tremble and stir
    from its place,
Hear ye, hear!—the threatening of His voice
    and the word—
How it leaps from His mouth!
Under the whole heaven we see Him,

His light on the pinions of the earth.

After Him rolls the thunder—

He thunders in the voice of His majesty—

But He followeth not the track—e'en though
His voice is heard.

Thus doth Omnipotence thunder—miracles in
His voice,

He doeth great things, though we notice not,

Speaketh to the snow, '' be upon the earth !''

'' And thou rain, be messenger of heaven !''

Verily the rain is the embassy of His power.

Upon the hand of every man He imprinteth
His seal,

Remembereth every member of His creation,

Gathereth the wild beasts in their lairs,

That they rest in their hiding-places.

Storms come from hidden recesses,

In its season icy coldness,

From the breath of God—He causeth frost,

And the broad watery expanse becometh firm.

When, also, bright rays dispel the mists

He is it, who scattereth the clouds by His
light.

He! Cause of all causes! In wisdom creative

He changeth them that they fit their pur-
pose.
All is as He biddeth it be for His world of
    men, for the earth,
For instruction, for earth-perfection, for love.
We find Him.'' (Job xxxvii.)

Therefore, one creator is! All else, everything which thou knowest, is the creation, the
revelation of this Only One! Everything is
from Him, and subject to Him, through Him
created, existing, active! And this world—
what may it be? We tread upon holy soil,
my Benjamin; we live in a divine world,
God's creature and servant is every being
around us! Every force is God's messenger;
every portion of matter given it by God to be
influenced, modified, and worked upon in accordance with God's omnipotent law. Everything serves God, each in its place, in its time,
with the quantity of forces and means given it,
fulfilling His word, contributing its share to the
work of the universe, which He joins together
to the whole perfect edifice—everything serves
God.

" He, who clotheth Himself with light
As with a garment;
Who spreadeth out the heavens as a carpet,
Who erecteth over the waters His arches,
Layeth the clouds at His feet,
Who walketh upon the wings of the wind,
He maketh the storms His messengers,
The flaming fire His servants." (Psalm civ.)

Servants are they all, the storm wind, the lightning, the rain, and the snow; a servant is the worm which crawls at thy feet, the blade of grass which nods to thee on the way, the thunder which rolls majestic above thee, and the cool breeze which fans refreshment to thy fevered cheek—all serve the Lord.

" For, as the rain and the snow descend from Heaven
And return not thither until they have moistened the earth,
And caused it to bear and yield fruit .
Until it have given seed to the sower
And bread to the eater;
Thus also is My word which cometh forth from My mouth,

It shall not return unto Me empty:

But it shall do that which I desire

And accomplish that for which I sent it forth.''

(Isaiah lv : 10, 11.)

All things are servants about the throne of God! '' For,'' say the sages, ''not with one creative word did the Almighty summon all things, the universe and the individual, into being, so that all should depend immediately upon His behest for its existence and activity, and that nothing should bear and uphold any other thing, but that all should be directly born and upheld by God alone. On the contrary, in a series of ten developments God called His world into existence, created an abundance of forces, and caused them to pervade each other, and influence each other, in accordance with His will—uniting and separating them in such a manner, that each should assist in maintaining the other; that none should contain alone the conditions of its existence and activity in itself, but should receive from fellow beings, and impart to fellow beings, the potencies

of life and work." [1] He, in His infinite
wisdom, ordained this mutual interdepend-
ence in order that each individual being
might contribute, with its measure of force,
whether much or little, to the preservation of
the All, so that whatsoever being should destroy, a fellow creature should thereby deprive
itself of a condition of its own life.   Thus
water, having penetrated the earth, is collected
in cloud, and sea; light, having pierced the
earthy crust and brought forth plants, children
of light and heat, is concentrated again into
sun, moon, and stars; the germ, offspring of
earth, is taken from the earth and given to the
crown of ripened fruit, which henceforth the
earth must receive that it give — thus one
glorious chain of love, of giving and receiving,
unites all creatures; none is by or for itself,
but all things exist in continual reciprocal
activity—the one for the All; the All for the
One.   None has power, or means, for itself; it
receives in order to give; gives in order to
receive, and finds therein the accomplishment

[1] "Ethics of the Fathers," chapter V, v. 1.

of the purpose of its existence. "ה,"
"Love," say the sages, "love which bears
and is born is the type of creation." "Love,"
is the message which all things proclaim to
thee.

FOURTH LETTER.

Man [1]—what is he in this God-filled world? What is his place in this throng of creatures of God, this choir of servants of the Lord? Though the Torah were silent, would not the contemplation of creation, would not your own breast tell you? Man, is he not also a creature of God? Should he not also be a servant of God? Every fiber of your body is a creation from the hand of God, formed by Him, arranged by Him, endowed by Him with power. Your spirit, that world of powers, is the creation of God from beginning to end. The divine spark, your personality, which, invisible as Deity, weaves and works in this microcosm, and under whose control stand intellect and body and the power to use the entire realm of nature for its purpose, this mysterious spritual force in you is itself emanation of Deity. Learn to deem yourself holy as creature of God and, while contemplating heaven and earth

---

[1] Genesis i : 27 and f.

and the great chorus of servants of the Lord,
consecrate yourself to your mission, and proclaim yourself with mingled solemnity and
joy, " servant of God ! " Since all things, the
smallest and the greatest, are God's chosen
messengers, to work, each in its place, and
with its measure of power, according to the
law of the Most High, taking only that it may
give again, should man alone be excluded
from this circle of blessed activity ? Can he be
born only to take ?—to revel in lavish plenty
or to starve in misery, but not to work ?—not
to fill any place, nor fulfill any purpose, but to
let all end in himself ? The world and all
which is therein serves God; is it conceivable
that man alone should only serve himself ?
No! Your consciousness pronounces you as
does the Torah, צלם אלהים " an image of
God." That is what man should be. Only
when working out some end canst thou know
God in love and righteousness; to work out
ends of righteousness and love art thou called;
not merely to enjoy or suffer. All which thou
possessest, spirit, body, human beings, wealth,

every ability and every power, they are means of activity; לעבדה ולשמרה to promote and preserve the world were they given—love and righteousness. Not thine is the earth, but thou belongest to the earth, to respect it as Divine soil and to deem every one of its creatures a creature of God, thy fellow-being ; to respect and love it as such, and as such to endeavor to bring it nearer to its goal, according to the will of God. For this reason every being impresses upon thy spirit an image of itself; for this reason thy heart-strings pulsate sym- pathetically with every cry of distress heard anywhere in creation, or with every tone of joy which issues anywhere from a gladsome being; therefore thou rejoicest when the flower blooms and sorrowest when it fades. *The law to which all powers submit unconsciously and involuntarily, to it shalt thou also subordinate thyself, but consciously and of thy own free will.* " *Knowledge and freedom,*" these words indi- cate at once the sublime mission and the lofty privilege of man. All forces stand as servitors around the throne of God, their capacity is hid-

den from themselves and covered are their coun-
tenances, so that they can not see the reason of
their mission, but they feel within them winged
power to act, and act in accordance with their
purpose. Thou, O man, thy countenance is half
uncovered, thy capacity is half revealed, thou
canst comprehend thyself as creature of God—
canst at least faintly appreciate the notion of
the mission which He breathed into thy ear;
canst thou see thyself encompassed round
about by God's active servants, canst thou feel
in thyself power to act and wilt thou not joyously join in the cry of the great chorus of
servants, נעשה ונשמע "we will do and
therefore hearken? We will obey, and fulfilling strive to comprehend the import of the
command!" Consciously and freely! Therefore thou shalt be first and highest servitor in
the company of servants!

Not by that which we gain, my dear Benjamin, can our vocation be determined, not
according to the extent of external or internal
possessions which we gather in external or
internal storehouses, should we estimate the

value of our lives; what we accomplish, what
results proceed from us, these should fix our
vocation, and in proportion as we use our
external and internal possessions to fulfill the
will of God and utilize every capacity, small
or great, for a truly human, God-serving
deed, will be the measure of our value. The
attainment of internal or external possessions
has only a value as the means of securing
ability for such activity. From the slightest
mental power and the nerve ganglia which
minister to it, to the executive force of your
hand with which you alter creation, and to
which the entire realm of nature is subject,
and every being which ever came within your
reach—all of these are means lent to you—
which one day will appear as witnesses for or
against you, before the throne of God, and
will testify whether you neglected or used
them well, whether you wrought with them
blessing or curse. There exists, therefore, an
external measure for the deeds of men, correspondence to the will of God—and an
internal measure for the greatness of men—

not the extent of powers conferred, not the
amount of results achieved, but the fulfillment
of the Divine will in proportion to the power
possessed. Life, therefore, may be an utter
failure in spite of the purest sentiments, if the
deeds done be not right; or may, on the other
hand, be most sublime despite infinitesimal
results, if the means did not suffice for more.
Happiness and perfection are, therefore, nothing but the greatest plenitude of external and
internal possessions which, only when employed in accordance with the will of God,
constitute the greatness of man. The angel
whose province it is to supervise the coming
into existence of man, says one of the sages,
takes the germ which is to be a human being,
brings it before the Holy One, blessed be He,
and asks, " This germ, what shall become of
it in life? Shall he that proceeds from it be
strong or weak, wise or simple, rich or poor?"[1]
He does not ask whether he will be good or
bad, pious or sinful, for all things depend
upon the decree of God, except virtue and the

---

[1] Treatise Niddah, page 16, B.

fear of the Lord, the pious reverence of heaven, these the Almighty leaves to the free will of men. Let us not, therefore, judge man according to that which is hardly half in his hands, but rather according to that which God put entirely into his control, and which, therefore, can alone constitute his greatness. The mission of mankind, thus comprehended, is attainable by all men, in every time, with any equipment of powers and means, in every condition. Whoever in his time, with his equipment of powers and means, in his condition, fulfills the will of God toward the creatures who enter into his circle, who injures none and assists every one according to his power, to reach the goal marked out for it by God—he is a man! He practises righteousness and love in his existence here below. His whole life, his whole being, his thoughts and feelings, his speech and action, even his business transactions and enjoyments—all of these are service of God. Such a life is exalted above all mutation.

Whether enjoyment or privation, whether

abundance or need be one's lot, whether tears
of resigned sorrow or joy exultant be shed—
the truly human personality, unchangeable
almost as Deity, sees in every gain or loss
only another summons to solve afresh the
same problem.   Thus man in his earthly frame
belongs to earth, and his terrestrial existence
is full of significance.   As no passing breath,
and no ephemeral grass-blade or butterfly
exists for nought, but furnishes its contribution, slight though it be, which God's wisdom
uses for the upbuilding of the All; thus also no
pleasure, no thought, no deed, trifling though
it be, is empty and purposeless; those which
are right are finished work delivered into the
hand of God that He may employ them for
the completion of His universe-plan.   Fulfillment of the Divine will with our property and
our pleasures, with our thoughts, words, and
deeds, that should be the contents of our lives.
And we should strive to ascertain this will.
For that is the special and peculiar greatness
of man, that whereas the voice of God speaks
in or *through* all other creatures, to him it

speaks directly that he accept voluntarily its precepts as propelling force of his life-activity. Go to, my Benjamin, and examine yourself; examine yourself in comparison with a grass-blade or a rolling thunder-peal, and if you do not, despite all your wealth of property and enjoyment of inner and outer possessions, blush with shame and veil your face in the presence of the angelic grandeur of such creatures, because of your selfish pettiness; and if you do not then rouse yourself with all your strength, with every spark of your being, to acquire for yourself such angelic power, then go and lament the degradation which the age has brought upon you.

"Bless, O my soul, the Lord,

And all my inner parts recognize His holiness!

Bless, O my soul, the Lord,

And forget not all which He lets ripen for
    thee.[1]

That He forgiveth all thy perversities,

That He healeth all thy ailings,

That He redeemeth from the grave thy life,

---

[1] גמל — to ripen.

That He crowneth thee with loving kindness
  and mercy,
That He satisfieth thee with good things, which
  adorn thee,
That thou mayest renew as the eagle thy
  youth.

.   .   .   .

Sunken man—as grass are his days,
As the flower of the field he bloometh;
The wind bloweth over him, he is no more,
No more doth his place know him.
But the loving kindness of the Lord is from
  eternity to eternity
Unto those who revere Him, and His mercy
  endureth unto the children's children,
Of those who regard His covenant,
And remember His commandments, to do
  them.
For He—who hath founded His throne in
  Heaven,
Ruleth in majesty throughout the All.
Bless Him, therefore, ye His messengers!
Ye who, girded with strength, fulfill His word
Obeying the voice of His word;

Bless Him, all ye His hosts!
His servants, fulfillers of His will!
Bless Him, all ye His creatures, in every place
  of His kingdom,
Bless also thou, O my soul, the Lord." [1]

---

[1] Psalm ciii.

FIFTH LETTER.

I had formed no different conception of you,
dear Benjamin, than your recent letter gave
me. What youth, still capable of enthusiasm
for the noble, could contemplate Heaven and
earth and their hosts, or could reflect upon
their work, or the work of any single creature,
without forming a notion of his task in life
consonant with his dignity as a human being,
or could do otherwise than to cast away with
shame and contempt the idols of silver and gold,
and particularly the universal idol, ''Pleasure?''
The object of such insight into the true mission of humanity, and of the consequent renun-
ciation of sensual enjoyments, is not, however,
indolent withdrawal from the active tasks of
life, but, on the contrary, manly vigor, and
the pursuit of the highest aims, using human
possessions and capacities, not, however, as
ends, but as means. The richer Heaven makes
you in internal and external possessions, the
more exhaustive fulfillment of His will He
demands of you; the wider-extended and all-

embracing does your duty become. You are right also in saying that the mere contemplation of the abilities of man is sufficient to prove it his duty to accomplish some end. Consider, furthermore, how his whole physical and intellectual constitution clearly indicates the tasks for the carrying out of which he is adapted; his head is borne proudly erect that his eyes may examine and inspect the world in which he moves; his hands are equipped with mobile fingers admirably fitted for the work of the artist and sculptor; his intellectual power is sufficient to know the things which shall serve him as means to his ends, but beyond that the path of knowledge is diffi· cult and dangerous, and pursued but by few; the development of his mental force is itself dependent upon external means, upon words and communications ; but, in contradistinction thereto, the heart, the source of all action, is capable of embracing all beings in regard and love, is capable of the greatest increase, of unlimited progress.

You are right also in asserting that, thus

understood, revelation of the Divine will is absolutely required, whether external or internal, or both. I am not at all surprised that you can not follow me in my Biblical interpretations. For the present, therefore, accept my outlined statements as though they were mere personal hypotheses of my own; investigate their intrinsic truth; familiarize yourself with the thought: "How would it be if this were really the contents of the Torah?" and leave it to me to demonstrate later that such is really the case. Let us now continue. We have now, guided by the Torah, ascertained the position of man in creation. Neither as god nor as slave shall he stand in the midst of the creatures of the earth-world; but as brother, as co-working brother, occupying, however, the rank of first-born among his brother beings, because of the peculiar nature and extent of his service; he is to be administrator of the whole Divine estate, the earth-world; to provide and care for all therein according to the will of God. From God alone, source of all *might*, does man derive the *right* to take for his own use the earth-world, but with this right comes also the *duty*, only to appropriate the *permitted*, and to use that in strict accordance with the will of the Giver. "Good" should be for him only that which agrees with this Divine will and with the disposition fixed for objects by Divine wisdom; "evil" only that which stands in opposition to these principles. Not that should be deemed good or evil which is agreeable or disagreeable to him, man; which is pleasant or unpleasant to his sensual nature, or that which harmonizes with, or is opposed to, principles, arbitrarily selected by himself without reference to the will of Deity.

For neither the gratification of impulses and lusts, nor ambitious self-aggrandizement and caprice constitute the task of man, but he shall elevate all his power, desires, and physical qualities to be means of carrying out the will of God, of bringing him nearer to his sought-for goal. Man's freedom, of course, postulates the possibility of mistakes and error.

Man has the duty to submit willingly to the

law which all others are compelled to obey,
and this naturally implies that he has also the
power to disobey it. Through his animal
portion, his body with its desires, he is
threatened with sensual lust; that, dazzled
by the charm of the pleasant sensations which
the Divine love has caused to accompany every
act of satisfying his needs, he may no longer
regard pleasure as the means but as the end
itself. Through the power of his intellect he
is threatened with pride, that because of his
ability to control material things, and to alter
them in accordance with a certain perceived
purpose, he may look upon himself as master,
forgetting thereby God the Lord, forgetting,
also, that all things are Divine possessions
lent him for specific purposes, and may usurp
to himself the right to subject all to the
domination of his own will. Deepest degradation may result when his entire effort is
devoted to the gratification of animal lust,
and the mind of the ruler lowers itself to be
the slave of the beast, employing all its skill
only to secure the gratification of bestial de-

sires. Then is man the most dangerous
beast of prey, for he is armed with intellect,
and the whole world is not safe against the
caprices of his passions.

Scripture omits to narrate any revelation of
God's will to mankind in general, as it re-
serves this for the later history of a special
nation, to which all which precedes but serves
as a guide and an introduction.[1]

One educational commandment appears,
and then man and his education by God are
shown. A world is laid at man's feet for him
to possess and enjoy, but one enjoyment is interdicted, without revealed reason, solely as a
decree of the Most High. For man should
subordinate himself to his Creator, and for
him highest wisdom consists in obeying the
will of God as the will of *his* God. But to be
willing to fulfill the behests of that will only
when or because they appear also to us right
and wise and good, could that be called
obedience to God? Would not that rather be

[1] Except one revelation given after the flood to the sons of
Noah.

obedience to oneself? Lust and désire for
pleasure tempt us with seductive words:
" How attractive it is, how agreeable, how
sweet ! " Pride of intellect adds also its contribution to the words dictated by desire:
" Have not we also mind, intelligence, and
understanding? Can we not, like gods, know
of ourselves what is good and what bad?
Why, nothing is easier ! How sweet it is, is
it conceivable that it should not be good?
Besides, unto us belongs the earth and the
fulness thereof ! " Thus only the sweet is re-
garded by man as good, as bad only the bitter.
The history of all sin is the same. God reveals Himself as Judge, but also as Father
and Teacher. Verily, judgment is His pre-
rogative, for does not the earth, and the fulness thereof, belong to Him? Have we not
received from, yea, from Him alone, power
and right to acquire and to enjoy ? If we mis-
use this power but once, stretch out our hand
but a single time toward that which is forbidden, have we not thereby forfeited all claim to
the right of existence on earth ? " On the day

when thou disregardest the prohibition, thou shalt surely forfeit thy life,'' is the warning of the just Judge. Nevertheless, God does not exact the incurred penalty of sin from His fallen child, but strives, with paternal love and forbearance, to guide him to the right.

The path to pleasure is made difficult to discourage the development of the animal side of his being and to render less arrogant his pride; that the real man in him be led upwards to God, through realization of the limitations of his power, and that something else must be his task and his greatness than that which can be thus easily conferred upon him, or taken from him. Thus also every one of us is taught even to-day. In our experience God's paternal teaching speaks to us. Into the realm of the temporal each one enters pure and capable of attaining to the highest stage of human greatness. That you are born in this particular hour, in this certain place, amid such and such surroundings, with your own special parents, brothers, and sisters, and with the definite measure of intellectual and physical powers

and material possession which you hold; that
you find certain teachers, acquaintances, and
friends, that is the Eden into which God puts
you.   But it is not given that you may in pride
forget Him and cling to temporal possessions
as tho they were the eternal good.   Do tLat
and sorrows צרות will enter into your life-
tabernacle, which will throw you back into
your own insignificance, and will forcibly in-
form you that all, parents and family, friends
and acquaintances, wealth and possessions,
body and soul, are but gifts—gifts of God, and
that you in yourself are not all.   You are here
to use every possession as an instrument put
into your hands to help you fulfill the will of
God.

But freedom delays the success of education.
Through labor pride is nurtured, and man
calls "his" the soil which he has moistened
with his sweat (קין) ; the necessity of pro-
viding for the satisfying of physical cravings,
which demand an increasingly large portion of
the good things of the world, exalts again the
animal in man; he sees in himself only an ani-

mal, and deems his mind only a means of procuring the gratification of physical desires; the
human in man sinks (נפילים.) That which
could lift him up, the acknowledgment of
God as the only Ruler and Father, and, therefore, of everything else as creature and servant,
and consequently of himself, as well as servant and child, this acknowledgment has
grown dim. For as soon as man ceases to
look upon himself as the empowered guardian
and administrator of the earth-world, as soon
as he endeavors to carry out, not the will of
God, but his own will, and ceases to be servant
of God; he sees no longer in the strength-
endowed beings around him the servitors of
Deity, but independent forces which seek possession, lust, and power, he has no eye any
more for the law of the All-One whom they
all serve, and the world divides itself for him
into as many gods as he sees forces in operation. For him the sun does not shine, nor the
thunder roll, the lightning flash, or the earth
deck itself in green; the storm roar, or the living beings reproduce their kind, because they

must, but because they wish, for the consciousness of the law is gone from his own breast.
He, therefore, desiring only possession and
lust, becomes a slave of the beings from which
he hopes to obtain that which he desires, he
bends the knee to the creatures (אנוש) until
finally, recognizing the omnipotence of his
passions, he deifies them; and, furthermore,
since all beings seem to him not servants of a
great world-plan, but independent forces, seeking power and lust, he soon ceases to look upon
the pursuit of power and lust as bestial and
unworthy of man, but deems it divine, man's
most worthy goal. The acknowledgment of
the All-One would lift him up, but polytheism
becomes the grave of his humanity. The generation seemed incorrigible, and—destruction
was its lot. Only one man, the father of a
family, who walked before the All-One, sought
righteousness, and elevated himself by govern-
ing sternly the animal in his nature, offered
consolation in this destruction of the generation. He was saved, with his family, to found
a new edifice of mankind נח.

SIXTH LETTER.

The new generation, which should have learned to recognize God in holy awe as Judge, Master, and Savior, forgot soon this lesson. In its pride it desires to establish itself as master upon the earth, just presented to it as a Divine gift. Because of the power with which it rules over nature, it believes that it can dispense with God in establishing and maintaining its new life. Thus begins history. God no longer wills the destruction of humanity, but its education. By experience He desires to train mankind to the knowledge of themselves and of Him. Humanity must not sink again to the deep degradation of the perished generation. Men must be dispersed, lest the human species slowly spreading over the earth form but a single family, and the corruption of one part be quickly communicated to the whole. They must be dispersed in order that mankind may

53

rejuvenate itself from its own midst, and when
one race has gone through all the stages of
the sinful illusions which weaken and corrupt
mankind, and is enervated, exhausted, and
unfit for the Divine purpose, it shall yield its
place to a stronger and hardier race, which
shall begin a fresher, purer life.

Mankind must be scattered, must distribute
itself among all the different regions of earth in
order that the most divergent and contrary faculties of the human mind may find in nature the
needed opportunities of development, in order
that experience become full and complete. In
order to render this plan of education possible,
the earth was reconstituted after it had been
laid waste and desolated; diversified as regards
its soil and climate, and divided into various
continents and lands, by seas and rivers,
mountains and deserts. This diversity of the
earth was, by the Divine plan, intended to
profoundly influence man, vainly fancying
himself master of the earth, and to affect, even
to their innermost characteristics, his body, his
opinions, his habits, his passions, and his

language. Thus should a broad and variegated experience become possible. This experience should make him worthy of God and of himself; should teach him to recognize the supreme dominion of God over nature and human life; should cause him to realize that the task of man is higher than merely to possess and to enjoy.

From this time on nation after nation enters into the arena of history; each presents some new power, some new capacity of the human intellect, and uses these faculties, in battle with nature and with each other, for the purpose of obtaining wealth and enjoyment. Gladly would the nations retain for all eternity what they have thus gained, but a higher hand, upon which the conditions of their success are dependent, dashes what they thought indestructible, by a slight breath of Divine potency, into ruins, and before the eyes of wondering humanity, it brings to pass from unnoticed trifles the most tremendous results. When a people has succeeded in climbing to the summit of material greatness, in its very

greatness, nay, even because of it, it crashes
down into destruction, and forsakes the sphere
of its activity for similar attempts on the part
of the succeeding generations. The time
must and will come when the inevitable results
of all these efforts will be clearly manifest to
the minds of the latest of men. Then, when
these attempts are finally completed, when
every nation in its rise and fall will have
inscribed in the book of history, as its judgment of human greatness, "הבל" "vanity
and folly;" when ruined are all efforts to attain lasting felicity by human possessions and
greatness, and crushed all the edifices of violence and the schemes of materialistic cun-
ning; when only that permanently endures
which men have based upon God-revering
righteousness and love; after mankind, which
had, in strange delusion, placed all creatures,
and even man himself, upon the throne of the
Most High, has learned, in the destruction of
human ambitions, the nothingness of these
puny rivals of Deity, and lifts its eye, unob-
scured by superstitious veil, to the All-One.

and comprehends again true human greatness,
to which wealth and lust are but means; when
this knowledge, this sentiment, pervades re-
united humanity; when men are ripe for the
question, not " what should we do in order to
be happy and blessed, but, when we are happy
and blessed, when we bear the fulness of good
in our hands, what shall we do with this
blessing ? " then

" At the end of days the mount of the Lord will
    be firmly established upon the peaks of the
    mountains,[1]
And born by the hills—and to it all peoples
    shall stream.
And there shall go great nations and speak:
" Come, let us go to the mount of the Lord,
    to the house of the God of Jacob,
And He will teach us His ways and we shall
    walk in His paths;
For from Zion shall come forth the law and
    the word of the Lord from Jerusalem."
He will judge between the nations, and teach
    mighty peoples,

---

[1] Isaiah, Chapter ii.

That they shall beat their swords to scythes
  and their spears to pruning-hooks,
That no people shall lift up the sword against
  another,
And they shall no more learn war.
O house of Jacob! Go before us, that we
  may also walk in the light of the Lord !
For thou hast forsaken thy people, O house of
  Jacob!
So that they filled themselves from the East,
Became time-servers, like the Philistines,
And satisfied themselves with things born of
  strangers.
And when His earth became full of silver and
  gold, and there was no end of treasures,
And when His earth became full of horses,
  and there was no end of chariots;
Then also did His earth fill with gods.
They bowed themselves to the work of His
  hands, to that which His fingers had formed.
Mankind sank then, humanity fell, and Thou
  didst not lift them up!
" Enter into the rock, hide yourselves in the
  dust,

Before the terror of the Lord, before the great-
    ness of His majesty.''
Thus will be lowered the eye of the haughti-
    ness of man,
Thus will be humiliated the pride of men,
And God alone will be great on that day.
For there is a day unto the Lord of Hosts
Concerning every proud and high thing, yea,
    concerning all the haughty
That they sink!
Concerning all the cedars of Lebanon, though
    high and exalted,
And concerning all the oaks of Bashan;
Concerning all the high mountains and all the
    elevated hills,
Concerning every high tower and every strong
    wall,
Concerning all the ships of Tarshish and all
    the edifices of lust;
That the pride of man may be bowed down
    and broken human haughtiness,
And that God alone may be great on that
    day;
The gods He will cause to disappear in smoke,

And people shall hasten into the clefts of
    rocks and the cavities of earth
From before the terror of the Lord and the
    glory of His majesty,
When He arises to rule the earth.
On that day man shall cast away the idols of
    his silver
And the idols of his gold,
Which have caused him to bow to the mole
    and the bat;
And will hasten into the fissures of the rocks
    and hollows of stone
From before the terror of the Lord and the
    greatness of His majesty
When he arises to rule the earth."

.   .   .   .

When you will have read through the pages
of history, with the " voice which gathers all "
you will exclaim—
" Vanity of vanities!   All is vain! [1]
What is the end of man with all his toil under
    the sun ?
Generations go, generations come, and the

---
[1] Ecclesiastes i : 2-15, and xii : 13.

earth-development marches ever to a hidden
   future;

Here rises fortune's sun, there it sinks, e'en
   while rising, and to its place of setting its
   course is turned;

Rises to midday strength—turns to midnight
   gloom—

Thus circles the day, and in its circling turns
   again to its beginning.

All nation-streams rush to the sea of death,
   but the sea is not filled; to the spot where
   the streams are born.

They return again to follow anew.

All words are powerless, man can not speak,

The eyes can not see enough, the ear not fully
   hear;

What was is what shall be, what was produced
   is what shall be produced;

All new is nought under the sun.

If thou speakest, "behold, this is new!" verily, in the ages of the past, it came into being.

There is no remembrance of the former ones,

Forsooth, of the latest there will be no remembrance.

Would I devote my heart to search
Yea, in wisdom to study all that is done under
    the sun,
Useless were the toil; God gave it to the chil-
    dren of man
For matter of thought, that they might busy
    themselves with it.
I see all that is done under the sun,
And behold, all is vanity and useless wearying
    of the spirit!
That which is perverse can not be straight-
    ened;
The imperfections can not be counted.
This is the conclusion of the matter,
After all has been heard.
God thou shalt revere, His mandate obey,
For in this is the whole task of mankind.''

   .   .   .   .   .   .

'' O Lord, a dwelling art Thou.   Thou abidest
    with us[1]
Though generation follow after generation;
Before the mountains were born, Thou brought-
    est forth the earth;

---

[1] Psalm xc : 1–7.

Even the inhabited world of men!

Yea, from hidden past to veiled future—omnipotent art Thou!

Degraded mankind thou lettest sink to destruction's verge,

Then speakest, "Return to human worth, O
children of man,"

For a thousand years are in Thy sight

As yesterday when it hath passed away,

E'en as a watch in the night.

Thou causest them to flow away with the
stream of life,

Sleep they become;

In the morning man is as the fresh grass,

In the morning he flourishes and blooms,

But at eventide he is withered and dry."

.   .   .   .

"O God! be gracious unto us, and bless us,[1]

Let Thy guiding light shine e'er upon us!

That there be known on earth Thy way,

Amongst all nations Thy salvation.

That the nations acknowledge Thee, O God,

Even the nations altogether.

---
[1] Psalm lxvii.

That the nations rejoice and be glad
When Thou judgest the people in righteous-
ness
And the nations Thou guidest on earth.
Selah!
May the nations acknowledge Thee, O God,
Even the nations all together,
When the earth shall have yielded its fruit,
God, even our God will bless us.
May God bless us and let fear Him
All the ends of the earth.''

.   .   .   .

'' Thus speaketh David, son of Jesse,[1]
Thus speaketh the man, high exalted,
Anointed of the God of Jacob,
Sweet singer of Israel.
The spirit of God spoke in me,
His word was on my tongue,
There spoke to me the God of Israel,
To me spoke Israel's rock.
Among mankind righteousness shall prevail,
The fear of God shall conquer.
When salvation's morn shall shine,

---

[1] Samuel II, xxiii : 1-7.

Bright as the sun it shall flash.
That morn shall know no cloud,
Radiant with light, fertile with rain,
Grass shall spring from the earth.
Is not thus my house with God,
For a concealed covenant of eternity He estab-
     lished unto me,
In all ordered and preserved.
All embracing is my salvation,
All embracing the goal,
Though it shine not yet forth.
But the deeds of violence,
Like scattered thorns are they all,
Removed by an unseen hand.
Would one assault them,
'Twould need sword and spear.
In fire unseen they shall be consumed,
Through invisible direction.''

SEVENTH LETTER.

From the beginning of the passage of Isaiah you have comprehended the place which Israel should occupy in the series of development of the nations, and have not erred, dear Benjamin.

While mankind, educated by experience, was to learn to know God and itself from its manifold vicissitudes, the final goal of this experience was to be made surer and speedier of attainment by a special ordainment. Because men had eliminated God from life, nay, even from nature, and found the basis of life in possessions and its aim in enjoyment, deeming life the product of the multitude of human desires, just as they looked upon nature as the product of a multitude of gods, therefore, it became necessary that a people be introduced into the ranks of the nations which through its history and life should declare God the only creative cause of existence, fulfillment

ᐟ of His will the only aim of life; and which
should bear the revelation of His will, re-
juvenated and renewed for its sake, unto all
parts of the world as the motive and incentive
of its coherence. This mission required for
its carrying out a nation, poor in everything
upon which the rest of mankind reared the
edifice of its greatness and its power; externally subordinate to the nations armed with
proud reliance on self, but fortified by direct
reliance on God; so that by suppression of
every opposing force God might reveal Himself directly as the only Creator, Judge, and
Master of nature and history.

Despite its political subordination, however,
this people was to receive from the hands of
its Creator all the means of individual human
and national prosperity, in order that it might
dedicate all its wealth of resources to the one
purpose—fulfilment of the Divine will. That
which universal mankind esteemed weal and
woe should also depend on the fulfilment of
this will, and thus even the external doings
and sufferings of this people should be a means

of directly inculcating a correct understanding
of God and human duty, which mankind
would otherwise have learned indirectly by
experience.

"One God, Creator, Lawgiver, Judge,
Guide, Preserver, and Father of all beings;
all beings His servants, His children, man
also His child and servant, from His hand all,
and this all to be used only for the fulfilment
of His will, since this alone is sufficient for a
proper attainment of the purposes of life, while
all other human occupations and pursuits are
but paths which lead to the goal of the fulfilment of the mission of humanity."

The proclaiming of these great truths was
to be the chief, if not the sole, life-task of this
people.

It must needs be a people which acknowl-
edges "ה" "The Ineffable Lord of Love," as
alone אלהים Omnipotent Master and Judge,
that is, which recognizes the God, who calls
and trains in love all mankind to His service,
as the only Founder, Guide, and Lever of its
thoughts. feelings, words, and deeds, which

knows that whatever it has is received from Him, and which, with all its power, lives for Him and Him alone.

A new stone was to be laid upon which could be built afresh the edifice of humanity, into which the knowledge of God and human duty might flee for refuge when rejected and disowned by others. It should be alike an example, a warning, a model, and an instruction.

Such a mission imposed upon it another duty, the duty of separation, of ethical and spiritual isolation. It could not join in the doings of the other peoples in order that it might not sink to their level and perish in the abyss of their worship of wealth and pleasure. It must remain alone and aloof, must do its work and live its life in separation, until, refined and purified by its teachings and its example, universal humanity might turn to God and acknowledge in Him the only Creator and Ruler. That attained, Israel's mission will have been accomplished.

"On that day the Lord shall be one and

His name one, for from Zion will go forth the
law and the word of the Lord from Jerusalem.''

"The Lord from Sinai came, from Seir shone
   He forth,[1]
Flashed from Paran's mount, with myriad
   holiness came.
At His right hand—a fiery law for them.
Verily He loved the nations,
But His holy ones were implements in thy
   hand.
When they shall follow in thy footsteps,
They, too, shall utter forth thy words;
The law, which Moses commanded unto us,
It is the heritage of the congregation of Jacob.''

[1] Deuteronomy, xxxiii : 2-4.

EIGHTH LETTER.

[1] In Abraham there was chosen as progenitor of this people a man who, in his individual life, already realized the ideal of the people that was to be. The All-One, whom he alone worshipped amidst the multitude of idolatrous seekers after wealth and lust, the All-One called and loving Him alone, Abraham cast from him his native land, his family, his parental dwelling, and all which man loves and cherishes, and followed Him who called him; he accepted the mission to become progenitor of a people from which " blessing should come to all the peoples of the earth which would keep the way of the Lord, to do righteousness and judgment," and followed Him; he carried out the ideal of this love to the All-One in his love to his children, to his fellow beings; he cared for them, saved them, instructed them, whenever and wherever he could, and prayed

[1] Genesis from chap. xii.

for them to the Judge of all. And He, for
whom he left all, and whose call he had followed into a strange land, He protected him
upon his wanderings, and blessed him, so that
he needed to derive safety and blessing only
from His hands, and used them only for the
salvation of the world.

To this "אהבה," love, was joined
"אמונה," faith and trust, firm as the immov-
able rocks, which beholds life sustained by the
All-One, and, therefore, holds fast to His
promises, however slightly the present may
seem to justify their expectation, and "יראה,"
that true fear of God which is ready any
moment to surrender uncomplainingly the
dearest to the Most High, because it realizes
that all man possesses is but the free-will
gift of God. These sentiments of the soul,
this conscientiously-scrupulous and pious view
of life, they were transmitted as an inheritance to Isaac, his son, and to Jacob, his
grandson, the former more prominently mani-
festing the qualities of the attribute of
"יראה," the latter those of "אמונה."

"They wandered from people to people, from one kingdom to another nation. He permitted no man to oppress them, but punished on their behalf princes, saying, "Touch not my anointed ones; do no evil unto my prophets." [1]

In the lives of these individuals God revealed Himself as the invisibly ruling Providence until they had grown to a family of seventy persons. In them was the kernel of the future nation. But the people which grew from this kernel was not spontaneously fitted for its sublime mission; it required to be trained, to be taught until it attained the capacity needed for its task. In contrast to other peoples it could find the proper preparation for its national duties only in the school of suffering. It needed to be deprived of all which constitutes ordinarily the glory of nations, even of that which makes the external splendor of individual men, it had to lose all but morality, religion, and hope, in order that it might receive all its life-treasures from Him alone.

Egypt, which at that time enjoyed the high-

---

[1] Psalm cv: 13-15.

est perfection of human culture, and which looked upon its soil and its river as its gods, Egypt became the cradle of misery in which Israel passed its infancy of preparation for its sublime mission. As reward for a benefit originating from one of them (Joseph), they were invited to make their home in the Nile-land, they were first guests, then citizens; but Egypt, revering only material possessions, knew not the All-One, saw not in all human beings His children, and in the arrogance of its power it treacherously disregarded the rights of hospitality and humanity, and made Israel its slaves. Israel sank to the lowest plane of human existence, though its numbers had increased to the proportions of a nation, and Mizraim, once a host, became unto it a tyrant, proud in its might, mocking and scorning the feeble and oppressed. Then appeared the All-One.

Upon a light cloud He appeared,
And there trembled Egypt's gods.

He revealed Himself as only Creator, as Lord of nature, though human hands had sought to master it, as God of nations, as Vindicator of the oppressed, as Judge of the arrogant. Mizraim's greatness sank before the majesty of the people which found its all in God. This God spoke—and there sank the walls of the Egyptian prison, and freed from its chains the people marched forth. From the hands of God it received freedom and nationality, and as object of this all, the revelation of His will as guidance for human life, the Torah. In Mizraim's school, in the education of the wilderness, "אמונה," faith and trust was to become the basal element of its character; it was to acquire that firmness of devotion to the All-One which should strengthen and console it in the manifold trials that were to come.

In the wilderness it received the Torah, and thus in the wilderness, without land or soil, it became a nation. It became a body, whose soul was the Torah, and, therefore, could be truthfully called "ממלכת כהנים," "a kingdom of priests," for as the priest in the midst of a single people was this nation to be in the

midst of universal mankind, preserving the
law of God, and practicing and fulfilling its
holy precepts.   " גוי קדוש,"   " Holy nation,"
was also to be its appellation, for, through the
fulfilment of the Divine law, it was to become
holy, not participating in the worldly doings
of other nations, but preaching the sacredness
of humanity by the example of its life.   The
Torah, the fulfilment of the Divine will, was
to be its soil and country, and aim; its national existence, therefore, was neither dependent upon, nor conditioned by transitory things,
but eternal as the spirit, the soul and the word
of the Eternal One.

It was to be a people in the midst of the peoples; as people it was to show the peoples that
God is the Source, and the Giver, of all blessing; that to dedicate oneself to the fulfilment
of His will means the attainment of all happiness that man can desire; that this sacred
resolve is sufficient to give stability and secu-
rity to human existence.   It received, therefore, the blessings of a land and state-power,
not, however, as end, but as means of carry-

ing out the Torah, its possession and retention dependent, therefore, upon fulfilment
thereof as only condition. It was to be separate, even in happiness, from the nations in
order that it might not learn of them to revere
well-being and fortune as the goal of life,
and, like them, sink into the worship of wealth
and lust.

How glorious a sight, this people, if it succeed in attaining its ideal! One God, the All-
One, one Lord and Father of them all; they
all equal brothers, subject to the paternal government of the All-One; the fulfilment of His
will in righteousness and love their only greatness, and in order to be able to successfully
accomplish their task, the Divine blessing
poured out unto them lavishly, without stint
or limitation.

" How goodly are thy tents, O Jacob,[1]
Thy tabernacles, O Israel!
As brooks they are stretched forth,
As gardens by the river,
As aloes, which the Lord hath planted,

---

[1] Numbers xxiv : 5-7.

As cedars by the water;
The water floweth from the vessels of God,
'Tis His seed by the rushing streams.
Therefore shall His king be exalted above
   Agag,
His kingdom shall be uplifted.
He saw no wickedness in Jacob,
He beheld no violence in Israel;
The Lord, his God, is with him,
And trumpet blowing, homage to the King.
The God, who led him forth from Egypt,
Is strength to him as the buffalo's mighty
   horns.
Therefore, no sorcery is in Jacob;
No wizard-art in Israel,
The time cometh when shall be sought
In Jacob and Israel what God hath wrought.''

NINTH LETTER.

Only for a short time was Israel able to attain its ideal, the fulfilment of its mission in prosperity. Even the first leader of the nation, Moses, foretold that upon God's soil they would forget God; that, led astray by the example of the other nations, they would esteem only wealth and pleasure worthy of seeking, and would become oblivious to their mission. There came the time when, even in Israel, the prophet could lament—"As the number of thy cities were thy gods, O Judah." It became necessary to take away the abundance of earthly good, the wealth and the land, which had led it away from its mission; it was obliged to leave the happy soil which had seduced it from its allegiance to the Most High; nothing should be saved except the soul of its existence, the Torah; no other bond of unity should henceforth exist except "God and its mission," which are indestructible, because spiritual. Through the annihilation

79

of Israel's state-life its mission did not cease,
for that had been intended only as a means to
an end.   On the contrary, this destruction
itself was a part of its fate; so strangely com-
mingled of divine and human elements, in
exile and dispersion its mission was to be
resumed in a different manner.   No other sins
had been committed in the Israel-state than
appear in the life of other nations, but that
which could be tolerated among others could
not be excused in Israel ; for its special office
was to preserve itself pure from all sin and
perversity, since " ה " was its God.   Destruction and misfortune are therefore no less instructive for Israel than prosperity.   The dispersion opened a new, great, and wide-extended
field for the fulfilment of its mission.·   But
before the great wandering through the ages
and the nations began, God gathered them
again upon their home-soil, as a father, who
is forced to send his children forth into the
world, gathers them together in his house
before their departure, to extend to them at
once his parental blessing and his fond fare-

well. There, in their national home, they
bound closer to themselves the Torah-bond
which henceforth was alone to join them
together. On the very eve of the exile, a
branch left the parent tree, which was obliged
to surrender largely the characteristics of the
parent stem, in order to bring to the world,
which had relapsed into polytheism, violence,
immorality, and inhumanity, the tidings of the
existence of the All-One and of the brotherhood of man and his superiority to the beast,
and to proclaim the deliverance of mankind
from the bondage of wealth-and-lust worship.
Assisted greatly by this offshoot in rendering
intelligible to the world the objects and purposes of Israel's election, the nation was
scattered into the four quarters of the earth,
unto all peoples and all zones, in order that in
the dispersion it might better fulfill its mission.

"To the wilderness again," proclaimed the
  Prophet's voice.

" Into the wilderness again ; prepare there the
  path of the Lord." [1]

---

[1] Isaiah, chap. xl : 3-5.

Make smooth in evening gloom a way for our
   God.
When every valley will be lifted ; when hill
   and mount are lowered ;
When the rough ground is smoothed ; when
   the ridges are made even,
Then will be revealed the glory of the Lord,
And all flesh shall see that the mouth of God
   hath spoken.''

Israel accomplished its task better in exile
than in the full possession of good fortune.
Indeed, improvement and correction were the
chief purposes of the *Galuth*—exile. With
its own eyes the nation saw the destruction of
the power and the splendor which had dazzled
it, and which it had begun to revere as its
gods. Could it ever again revere wealth,
power, and grandeur as the gods of life?
Without power, without splendor, without
brilliant show of human grandeur, it preserved its faithfulness toward the All-One and
the spirit and the maintenance of its only rescued treasure, the Torah—preserved it alive
imidst suffering and agony, enabled it to

endure all the blows of savage fanaticism unchained.

On every side states in all the glory of human power and pride disappeared from the face of the earth, while Israel, upheld only by its fidelity to God and His law, maintained successfully its existence. Could, then, Israel refuse to acknowledge this All-One as its God, or to accept His Torah as its only mission on earth?

And, in very truth, it proved that this training was not in vain. A thousand times delusions, armed with material power and passions aroused by these delusions, opened to Israel the path to the full enjoyment of earthly happiness, if it would, with but a single word, declare its rejection of the All-One—its disregard of His Torah; but, as often as temptation met it, it would cast away in scorn this easy key, preferring rather to extend the neck to the blow of the executioner. It sacrificed its own scanty measure of happiness, the most precious possession of earthly existence, wives, children, parents, brothers, and sisters,

life, property, and all the joys of life. With
Israel's heart-blood is written on all the pages
of history the doctrine that there is but one
God, and that there are higher and better
things for mankind than wealth and pleasure.
Its entire Galuth history is one vast altar,
upon which it sacrificed all that men desire
and love for the sake of acknowledging God
and His law. Among all nations and in
every region such altars have smoked. Did
they not teach, could they fail to teach, a
most impressive lesson? Deeply upon the
heart of Israel they impressed the conviction
that a more than human power was sustaining
them in their unparalleled tribulations. In
this power they learned to worship the All-
One; in faithful devotion to Him, they recognized their mission.

And now that these altars have ceased to
smoke, and the scattered ones of Israel are
tolerated, protected, even accepted as citizens,
how beautiful, nay, how necessary were it that
they should, in accordance with the permission
of the nations, develop in peace and quietude

all the grandeur of the Israel life. How beautiful it would be if Israel, obeying the word of its
prophet, should attach itself closely to every
state which has accepted its children in citizenship, and should seek to promote the welfare and the peace thereof.

If in the midst of a world which reveres
wealth and lust, it should live a tranquil life
of righteousness and love ; if, while everywhere the generation is rapidly sinking into
sensuality and immorality, Israel's sons and
daughters should bloom forth in the best
adornment of youth, purity and innocence; if,
though everywhere the habitations of men
should cease to be the orchards in which are
grown human fruit pleasing in the sight of
God and man, every Israelitish house should,
nevertheless, be a temple of true faith in God,
of reverence and love for Him ; if, though
everywhere avarice, lust, and greed should
become the motives of human actions, every
Jew should still, in despite thereof, be a silent
example and teacher of universal righteousness and universal love—if thus the

dispersed of Israel should show themselves
everywhere on earth the glorious priests of
God and pure humanity, O my Benjamin,
if we were, if we would become, what we
should be—if our lives were a perfect reflection
of our law—what a mighty engine we would
constitute for propelling mankind to the final
goal of all human education! More quietly, but
more forcefully and profoundly, would it effect
mankind than even our tragical record of sorrows, powerfully though this latter teaches the
intervention of providence in human affairs.

In the centuries of passion and scorn our
mission was but imperfectly attainable, but the
ages of mildness and justice, now begun,
beckon us to that glorious goal ; that every
Jew and every Jewess should be in his or her
own life a modest and unassuming priest or
priestess of God and true humanity. When
such an ideal and such a mission await us, can
we still, my Benjamin, lament our fate?

" Be pure, O ye that bear the weapons of the
Lord,'

---

¹ Isaiah, chap. lii : 11 ; chap. lvi : 7.

For not in lightness should ye go forth,
Nor in carelessness should ye walk ;
For He that walketh before you is the Lord,
And He that guardeth you is the God of
  Israel.
Behold, if my servant be but wise,
He shall be high and exalted and very great.
As many were amazed at thee,
Saying, "His appearance is corrupted from
  manly semblance,
His likeness from the children of men."
So shall light come to many peoples,
And kings shall close their mouths,
For what was not told unto them they shall see,
And what they never heard they shall con-
  template.
Wondering, they shall say, "Who would
  believe our report?"
"The arm of the Lord, upon whom is it re-
  vealed?"
He rises as a sapling before him
And as a root from arid land.
He had nor form nor beauty that we should
  see him,

Nor comeliness that we should desire him.
He was despised and forsaken of men ;
A man of sorrows, acquainted with sickness.
And when God hid His face from him,
We despised him and considered him not.
Yet 'twas but sickness from us he bore ;
Pains we had inflicted were his burden,
And we deemed him plagued,
Stricken of God and afflicted.
But he, though stricken through our sins,
Though crushed through our iniquities,
The bond of our peace he took upon him,
And in his congregation was healing for us.[1]
We all had gone astray as sheep ;
Each one had turned to his own way ;
But the Lord afflicted only him—
Smote him for the sin of us all.
He was oppressed, was harshly persecuted,
Silent endured and opened not his mouth.
As a sheep to the slaughter he was led,
As a lamb before the shearers was he dumb,
Nor opened he his mouth.
Of kingly rule and judgeship was he deprived,

---

[1] The Hebrew for "stripe" is חַבּוּרָה not חֲבוּרָה

And his fate, who could tell it?
For he was cut off from the land of life,
Through the sin of the nation came affliction
    unto him.
The wicked brought him to the grave,
The great and wealthy to his death,
Though violence he had never used
And deceit was not in his mouth.
But the Lord had willed his affliction and sick-
    ness,
That he should yield himself as guilt offering,
(Nevertheless destruction was not God's plan,
    but that)
He should see posterity, prolong days,
And the purpose of the Lord through his hand
    should be fulfilled.
Through suffering he should gain insight,
Should learn to be content,
And with this knowledge propagate the right
And do My service unto the many whose sins
    he bore.
Therefore shall I give him a portion among
    the many,
With mighty ones booty shall he yet divide,

Because he laid bare to death his soul,
And with sinners suffered himself to be counted,
Whereas he had borne the sin of many
And for sinners suffered himself to be stricken.''

.   .   .   .

'' Shout gladly, O barren one, that hath never
   borne,
Break forth in gladsome shouting and rejoice,
Thou that hath never known the pains of
   child-birth,
For more are the children of the desolate one
Than of her that hath a husband, saith the
   Lord.
Make broad the space of thy tent,
The curtains of thy dwellings, let them ex-
   pand,
Keep them not back;
Make long thy cords, thy pegs make firm,
For to the right and to the left shalt thou
   spread forth.
Thy seed shall inherit nations,
And desolate cities they shall inhabit.
Fear not, thou shalt not be put to shame,
Be not abashed, for thou shalt not grow pale.

For the shame of thy youth thou shalt forget,
The disgrace of thy widowhood no more re-
member.
For thy Lord and thy Creator, "Reconciler
of Contradictions" is His name,
And thy Redeemer, the Holy One of Israel,
God of the whole earth is He called.
For as a wife forsaken and sad, the Lord re-
calls thee,
And as to the spouse of youth, once rejected,
does thy God speak.
For a short moment I forsook thee,
But with great love I take thee back.
In overwhelming wrath I hid my face a mo-
ment from thee,
But in everlasting mercy I have compassion
upon thee,
Saith thy Redeemer, the Lord.
For as Noah's flood is this unto me ;
For as I swore that Noah's flood should no
more come to pass,
Thus have I sworn no more to be wroth with
thee,
No more o'er thee my anger hot to pour.

Though the mountains should be movec
And the hills be shaken,
My mercy from thee shall not be moved,
And my covenant of peace shall not be shaken,
Saith He that hath compassion with thee, the
    Lord.
O thou poor, storm-driven one, unconsoled,
Behold, in rare clay shall I set thy stones,
With sapphires will I build thy fundaments.
Of crystal shall I make thy windows
Of flashing carbuncles thy gates,
And all thy boundary-walls of precious jewels.
And all thy children shall be disciples of the
    Lord
And great shall be the peace of thy children.
Only through righteousness canst thou be
    established ;
Keep far from oppression, for thou needst not
    fear,
From terror, for it will not come nigh unto
    thee
None shall fear aught but me, who, therefore,
    among thee
Could fear that aught would befall thee?

Verily, I have created every artizan
That bloweth in the fire the coal
And bringeth forth a tool for his work;
I have created every destroyer
That begetteth evil and harm.
But no weapon, formed against thee, shall
    succeed,
Every tongue that riseth 'gainst thee in judg-
    ment, thou shalt refute ;
This is the inheritance of the servants of the
    Lord
And of those whose righteousness is from me,
    saith the Lord.
All ye that are thirsty, come to the water,
Ye that have no silver, come, buy and eat ;
Come, buy without silver and without price
Wine that revives and milk that nourisheth.
Why weigh ye out silver for that which is not
    bread,
Your earnings for that which satisfieth not ?
Hearken unto me and eat that which is good
And may your soul be delighted with fatness.
And I will make with you an eternal covenant,
Even the ever faithful love of David.

For, behold, I gave him as a witness to the
     peoples,
Communicating and enjoining duty to the
     nations.
Behold, a people, which thou knowest not,
     thou wilt call,
And nations, that know thee not, unto thee
     will hasten,
Even to the Lord thy God, to the Holy One
     of Israel, that maketh thee beautiful.
Seek ye the Lord, the ever present;
Call upon Him, the ever near.
Let the passionate forsake his way,
The man of violence his counsel,
Let him return to the Lord,
He will have compassion upon him;
Even to our God for He doth much forgive.
Verily, my thoughts are not your thoughts
And your ways are not my ways, saith the
     Lord.
For as the heavens are high above the earth,
Thus are my ways high above your ways
And my thoughts above your thoughts.
For as the rain and the snow fall from heaven

And return not thither again
Until it has watered and made it bear
And caused plants to spring forth ;
Thus also my word, which goeth forth from
 my mouth,
Shall not return empty unto me
Until it has done what I desired
And accomplished that for which I sent it.
In joy shall ye go forth, in peace return,
Mountains and hills shall greet you with joy-
 ful shouting
And all the trees of the field shall clap their
 hands ;
Beneath the thorn-bush the cedar shall rise ;
Beneath the thistle the myrtle shall spring
 forth ;
Shall remain, as glory to the Lord,
Reminder of hidden time, shall nevermore be
 uprooted.
Thus hath the Lord said, "Take heed of jus-
 tice !"
Practise righteousness ; then will my salvation
 soon come,
My righteousness then will soon be revealed.

Happy the man that practises this,
The son of Adam that holds fast to it,
Who gives heed to the Sabbath that he profane
    it not,
Gives heed to his hand that it do no evil.
Neither should the stranger, that joins him-
    self to the Lord,
Say, " Verily, the Lord will separate me from
    His people ; "
Nor should the childless speak, " I am a dry
    tree ! "
For thus saith the Lord to the childless ones
    who keep my Sabbaths,
Who choose what I desire and hold fast to my
    covenant,
" Verily, I shall give them in My house, within
    My walls,
A place and a name, better than sons and
    daughters,
A name eternal, which shall never be cut off;
And the sons of the stranger, who join them-
    selves to the Lord
To serve Him, to love the name of the Lord,
Even to be unto Him as servants.

Whosoever gives heed to the Sabbath, not to
    profane it,
Whosoever holdeth fast to my covenant,
I shall bring them all to My holy mountain,
I shall cause them all to rejoice in My house
    of prayer,
Their burnt offerings and sacrifices shall be
    pleasing upon My altar,
For My house, a house of prayer shall it be
    called for all the nations.

TENTH LETTER.

My light and sketchy brush-strokes have
succeeded in reconciling you to the fate of
your people ; nay, more, you are happy that
you belong to this people, in spite of its pov-
erty and lowliness—even because of them.
What a glorious resulting of our correspondence, dear Benjamin ! But, when you conceive
yourself exalted to the lofty summit of the
idea of our mission and look upon the Law,
which has as ostensible purpose the realization
of this idea, you feel as though a yawning
chasm intervened between you and it. You
can not repress a feeling of sorrowing disap-
proval, a sensation of protesting wonderment
when you think, that *that* is supposed to be
the will of God ; nor do you see any real task,
any ideal work to which you are called,
nothing but praying and a passively-contem-
plative life, and in addition, unreasonable demands and senseless practices. But what

would you say, dear friend, if I were to tell
you that the excessive pressure of centuries
in its accumulated weight had finally only permitted the rescue of the externals of the Law,
but that the spirit had no longer found room?
What if I were to say that Israel, banished
from the society of the rest of mankind,
estranged from the world and its life, had lost
contact and sympathy with the world and life,
and no longer considered them in comprehending and interpreting the Law, but deemed
itself fortunate to have rescued even its, the
Law's, externals? Suppose I were to tell you
that a dull and prosaic dialectic had reduced
to merest mummies laws full to overflowing of
life and spirit, and that Israel, concerned and
apprehensive because of the errors and evils
which it had often seen follow the efforts of the
uncontrolled intellect, had driven it away from
the Law as one drives away a bird of prey
from a dearly-beloved corpse? Centuries of
oppression and misery, which offered no
opportunity for activity, which made patient
endurance and resignation the sole duties;

when only prayer could give strength, and
passive contemplation afforded the only consolation for the ills of life, must they not of
necessity depress the spirit and compel the development of the narrow and restricted? If,
furthermore, we say that the literary sources
of Judaism, in which its spirit is contained,
being misunderstood and misinterpreted, themselves aided in corporealizing and disguising
the spirit; that a perverted intellect comprehended the institutions which were designed
and ordained for the internal and external
purification and betterment of man as mechanical, dynamical, or magical formulas for the
upbuilding of higher worlds, and that thus
the observances meant for the education of the
spirit to a nobler life were but too frequently
degraded into mere amuletic or talismanic per-
formances; would you not admit, after all
this, dear Benjamin, that you know only external Judaism, only an unrecognized, uncomprehended, misunderstood Judaism, and even
that in a most fragmentary and incomplete
form?

Forget whatever you know of Judaism,
listen, as though you had never heard aught
concerning its teachings, and you will not only
be reconciled to the Law, but you will be filled
with genuine love for it and willingly will you
permit your whole life to be an expression and
manifestation of this Law.

I shall give you now only fundamental
principles, general outlines of the component
parts of the Jewish doctrinal system, hardly
anything but the nomenclature of terms and
concepts, and shall leave both elucidation and
demonstration for the future. Read my statements as though they were but hypotheses,
but they are none.

Every opinion which I shall express is the
result of many years' study of שׁם, תנ״ך and
מדרש;[1] every detail and every step finds its
corroboration in the Gemara, if this latter be
but comprehended according to the true meaning of its words and if, at every point, we put
to ourselves the questions, "What have I
heard here?" "What is the underlying con-

---

[1] Bible, Talmud, and Midrash.

cept of this statement?"   "What its purpose?"   "What the object of this symbolical
act?"   "What its natural meaning under the
given conditions and purpose?" We must,
furthermore, carefully distinguish between
דאורייתא[1] and דרבנן[2], and seek to comprehend the former by comprehending the essence
and nature of the thing enjoined, and the latter by making clear to ourselves the steps and
means required for the proper carrying out and
fulfillment of the Biblical law; nor must we
omit to take account of the peculiarities of
the original, which, having been intended pri-
marily for oral transmission only, and not to
be put into written form, which was expressly
interdicted as a matter of principle, gives only
the special rule, adapted for immediate application, but omits the universal, the spirit,
leaving that for direct individual instruction or
personal effort to ascertain.

After what has been now explained, I ask
you, what do you expect in the Torah? You

---

[1] Biblical ordinances.

[2] Rabbinical ordinances.

will answer, revelation of conduct, how you,
using the powers and faculties which are
yours, may fulfill the will of God towards the
beings by whom you are surrounded ; in other
words, how you may practise justice and love
with all and towards all.

Add to this also the idea of the mission of
Israel as a people called not only to accomplish the fulfillment of these principles in life,
but also to preserve and propagate their
theoretic concepts for its own education and
that of others. Join to it, furthermore, the
laws and ordinances which derive their origin
naturally from the state-life Israel once led
and which, in the absence of land and state,
became inapplicable, and you have the essential
binding contents of the Torah. [1]

(1) תורות. *Instructions or doctrines.* The
historically revealed ideas concerning God,
the world, the mission of humanity and of

[1] It is customary to divide the Mitzvoth in עשה and ל"ת,
commands and prohibitions, but this is not essential for our
purpose, for the same command may be, from one point of
view, positive, from another, negative. *E. g.* לא תעשוק and
לא יאכל חמץ and תאכל מצות or ביומו תתן שכרו

Israel, not as mere doctrines of faith or
science, but as principles to be acknowledged
by mind and heart, and realized in life. (2)
משפטים. *Judgments.* Statements of justice
towards creatures similar and equal to yourself, by reason of this resemblance and equal-
ity, that is, of justice towards human beings.
(3) חקים. *Arbitrary statutes.* Statements
of justice towards subordinate creatures by
reason of the obedience due to God; that
is, justice towards the earth, plants, and
animals, or, if they have become assimilated
with your personality, towards your own
body and soul. (4) מצות. *Commandments.*
Precepts of love towards all beings without distinction, purely because of the bidding of God and in consideration of our
duty as men and Israelites. (5) עדות.
Symbolic observances. Monuments or testi-
monies to truths essential to the concept of
the mission of man and of Israel. These tes-
timonies are symbolic words or actions which
bear a lesson for the individual Jew, collective
Israel, or mankind in general. (6) עבודה.

Service or worship. Exaltation and sanctification of the inner powers by word-or-deed symbols to the end that our conception of our task be rendered clearer, and we be better fitted to fulfill our mission on earth.

As basal principles to these grand divisions of religion we have three concepts, justice, love, and education.

(1) Justice, that is, consideration for every being as creature of God, for all possessions as arrangements willed by God, of all governments and systems as ordained by God and fulfillment of all duties towards them incumbent upon us.

(2) Love, that is, kindly acceptance of all beings as children of God, as brethren; promotion of their welfare, and the endeavor to bring them to the goal set for them by God, without motive or benefit, but simply to fulfill the Divine will and command.

(3) Education, that is, the training of oneself and others to such work by taking to heart these truths as life-principles, by holding them fast and preserving them for one-

self and for others, and by endeavoring to regain them whenever the influences of worldly
life have torn them from our possession.

Let us now go through them in detail and
endeavor to comprehend each in the light of
the principles upon which it is established.

ELEVENTH LETTER.

Toroth.—*Instruction or doctrines.*—Manifold
are the lessons which these important
constituents of the Divine system teach
us. They comprise the instructions derived from the historically-revealed manifestations of Divine truth and which it is our
duty to elevate into principles of our life. [1]
They teach us to know God in his unity and
as summoning us to comprehend our existence
in all its many-sidedness and to unite all our
powers, abilities, and conditions in subordination to the One. [2] They teach the active
service-duty of all beings, including man, who
must learn to look upon himself as one of the
host of ministering attendants of Deity and
willingly join their ranks. [3] His will in this
respect is revealed as unchangeable for all
ages. [4] Our experience is to serve us as

---

[1] Ex. xx : 2. [2] Deut. vi : 4; iv : 39; Ex. xx : 3; Deut xviii : 13;
Deut. xix : 26. [3] Deut. iv : 19, 20. [4] Deut. iv : 9; v : 19.

107

education; [1] the fear of God is to be taught us by the recognition of His illimitable greatness, the love of God by consideration of His unending mercy and kindness, unshakeable trust in Him by appreciation of His eternal faithfulness. [2]

They furthermore tend to ennoble thy inner character that it become pure and free of all that could drag thee down from the high pinnacle of thy holy mission. [3] They bid thee put aside pride and desire of sensual pleasure,[4] to respond sympathetically to the sorrow or joy of all beings, and to embrace them all in thy love as children of thy God.[5] These injunctions are but the applications of the principles demonstrated as true in the revelations given in the actions, in the mighty deeds, of God. His commandments are but the expressions of these principles; revealed as concepts, not as mere incomprehensible behests; whosoever desires truth will accept them.

[1] Deut. viii : 2. [2] Deut. vi : 12, 13 ; iv : 40; vi : 16; vii : 19. [3] Deut. x : 12-16; Lev. xi : 44, 20, 7. [4] Deut. viii : 11; Deut. v : 18. [5] Deut. xv : 17; Lev. xiv : 18.

Mishpatim. — *Judgments or Principles of Justice.*—All these ideal theories have only value, however, if thou really livest, as thou hast gained the conception, in a Divine world, with Divine powers, man-Israel. The first requisite is, *Justice!* Respect every being around thee and all that is in thee as the creation of thy God; everything belonging to them as given them by God or in accordance with law which He has sanctioned. Leave willingly to each being that which it is justly entitled to call its own. Be not as regards aught a curse. Especially honor every human being as thy equal, regard him in his essence, that is to say, in his invisible personality, in his bodily envelope and in his life.[1] Extend the same regard to his artificially enlarged body, his property;[2] to the demands which he may be entitled to make upon you for assistance by grants of property or acts of physical strength;[3] in measure and number;[4] in re-

[1] Exod. xx : 13; Deut. xxv : 1; xxvii : 24. ר"י,מ"ח [2] Lev. xix: 11, 13; Exod. xxii : 1; Lev. v : 21; Deut. xxiv : 14. ח"מ [3] Lev. xxv : 14; Exod. xxii : 6, 9, 13. ח"מ [4] Lev. xix : 35 ; Deut. xxv: 13. ח"מ

compense of injury to his person or posses-
sions.¹ Have regard, also, to his rightful
claim of truth;² of liberty, happiness, and
peace of mind,³ of honor and undisturbed
tranquillity.⁴ Do not abuse his weakness of
heart, mind, or body;⁵ do not unjustly employ thy legal power over him.⁶

Chukkim.—*Arbitrary or apparently inex-
plicable Statutes.*—The same thoughtful regard
which you show to man, show as well to
every lower being; to the earth which bears
and sustains all; to the world of animals and
plants, to your own body, to your own mental
faculties, to your " ego," that which is most
of all your own. It is the same justice which
you owe to other human beings. What in the
case of the Mishpatim results from the concept of identical personality, flows here from
the fundamental notion of equal subordina-

---

¹ Exod. xxii : 4, 5, 21, 33, 35; Deut. xxii : 8; Exod. xxi: 18. ח״מ
² Exod. xxiii : 7; Lev. xix : 11. ח״מ,ח״א   ³ Exod. xxii : 20; Lev.
xix : 34; Lev. xxv : 16; Lev. xix : 18. ח״מ   ⁴ Lev. xix: 16; Deut.
xvii : 5. ז״ו   ⁵ Lev. xix : 14; Deut. xxvii : 18; xiii : 12. ח״א,ח״מ,ז״ו
⁶ Exod. xx : 14; Lev. xix : 15; Exod. xxiii : 1, 6, 8 ; Deut. i : 16,
ח״מ.

tion to God, who defends all which is lower
in order and subject to you against your
caprice and the ebullitions of unregulated
will. Your duties towards humanity are more
intelligible to you simply because you have
only to think of yourself, your own views
and feelings, in order to recognize and sym-
pathize with the demands and needs of your
fellow-man. Could you put yourself as
thoroughly in the place of other beings, could
you even understand the conditions of the
union and the combined activity of your own
body and soul, you would find it as easy to
comprehend Chukkim as Mishpatim. They
ask of you to regard all beings as God's possessions; destroy none; abuse none; waste
nothing; employ all things wisely;[1] the kinds
and species of plants and animals are God's
order; mingle them not.[2] All creatures are
servants in the household of creation.[3]
Respect even the feelings and desires of

---

[1] Deut. xx : 19; Lev. xxii : 24. מלכים ה״ל יח״ר, ר׳׳ד, ס׳׳ן of the ר׳׳ד
Talma שבת, p. 67. א״ח [2] Lev. xix : 19; Deut. xxii : 9, 11.
[3] Deut. xxii : 6; Lev. xxii : 28. ר״ד.

beasts.[1] Respect the body of man even when the personality has departed.[2] Respect your own body as receptacle, messenger and instrument of the spirit.[3] Limit and subdue your impulses and animal actions under the law of God that they be used in a manner truly human and holy for the upbuilding of the holy purpose of the human race, that man sink not into a mere beast.[4] Respect your soul in nourishing your body; give the latter only so much and such food as will permit it to be a pure, obedient messenger of the world to the soul, of the soul to the world, but not such as to produce sluggishness or sensuality.[5] Therefore conceal and elevate, do not esteem too highly thy animal part, in order that in the end all contradictory dispositions be eliminated from you, and even the beast-like become truly human.[6] Finally, respect yourself in your purest emanation, your word.[7]

---

[1] Exod. xxiii : 5. חי״מ א״ח [2] Deut. xvi : 22. ד״י [3] Gen. ix : 5; Deut. iv : 9. חי״ד ד״י [4] Deut. xxiii : 10; Lev. xviii : 4-24. [5] Lev. xi; Deut. xiv. [6] Lev. xxiii : 10; Num. xxi : 21. [7] Num. xxx : 2 ד״י

TWELFTH LETTER.

Mitzvoth.—*Commandments.*—The next requirement, which, though second in rank,
gives life its completion and perfection, is love.
Never be the instrumentality of curse or misfortune to yourself or your neighbor, but
strive, like Deity, to do all your deeds in love,
and thus become a blessing to yourself and
your surroundings.[1] First become a blessing
to yourself in order that you may become it
to others. Seek to equip yourself with all
the capacities and means which can be of good
service to the welfare of your fellow beings;
make yourself rich with abundant store of
good and noble principles, and then devote
yourself to the world for perfect service of
blessing. To become the means of blessing,
learn first to honor your parents as messengers
of God, mankind, and Israel to you;[2] learn

---

[1] Deut. xxviii : 9; xiii : 4. [2] Exod. xx : 12; Deut. v : 16; Lev.
xix, 3.

also to revere wisdom, age, and virtue, as
guides and models, wherever and whenever
they appear realized in human character.[1]
Illuminate yourself with the revealed wisdom
of the Torah,[2] avoid the evil and seek the
good.[3]

Strive ever to draw nearer to God, to be
more closely united to Him in love and piety,
more devoted and faithful to thy sacred mission on earth.   Strive also to make the earth
a truly human habitation, its creatures truly
human possessions, in order that, in addition
to your internal resources you may acquire
also external wealth as means for carrying out
your mission of blessing, and in order to be
able independently to establish a house, as a
temple in which shall be reared young scions
of Adam's race as ideal human beings, ideal
Israelites.[4] For such purpose, to grace such
a house, take a wife and bring her into your
home.[5] Next follows the first task of your
blessed mission of love, the first and the

---

[1] Lev. xix : 32. ד״ן [2] Deut. v : 1 ; iv : 5. [3] Deut. xiii:5; xiii : 8.
[4] Genesis i : 28; Deut. xxxiv : 1. [5] Deut. xxv : 5; viii : 3. ד״ן, ח״א

highest; to be all in all to helpless human creatures without claim or demand upon you; even to sacrifice your own welfare in order that they shall be able to attain to both earthly well-being and spiritual ideal; that your child may become man-Israel.[1]

Your mission, however, is not limited by the walls of your house; beyond their limits you must assist with every particle of your strength wherever it is necessary to save the life, the property, or the happiness of a human being,[2] to assist the enterprise of a fellow man with your strength or fortune,[3] or to help suffering creatures of the lower order[4] wherever you can, by the use of your wealth, your physical or intellectual strength, or your word, support the needy, clothe the naked, feed the hungry, console the mourning, heal the sick, care for the unprovided, advise those in need of counsel, teach the ignorant, reconcile those sundered by anger and quarrel — in a word,

---

[1] Deut. xxxiii : 4; iv: 9; vi : 6; xi : 17. ד״א, ח״ח [2] Lev. xix : 10; Deut. xxii : 1. [3] Exod. xxiii : 5. ח״ם א ח״ח [4] Deut. xxii : 4; Exod. xxii : 5; ii : 22, 24; Lev. xxv : 35. ם ח ד״י

to be a blessing whenever and wherever you can.[1]

You must not only yourself fulfill these requirements, but see to it, also, that the sources be preserved from which you and your contemporaries and posterity may derive enlightenment and incitement for such life and work—*Torah-preservation.*[2]

Nor should you remain alone and isolated; join yourself to a community, by which alone your work can be made universal and eternal in its results; on the one hand, the congregation,[3] on the other, the state which harbors and protects you.[4] Living thus, you will contribute your share to *sanctifying the Divine name.* You will become monument and witness to the sway of God and the duty of man; your Israelitish and non-Israelitish brethren as well, will derive enlightenment and courage from your example, and will learn to serve the only God as their God, and to love Him with

---

[1] Deut. xxiii : 9, 15, 7; Lev. xix : 17; Deut. vi : 18.　[2] Deut. xxxi: 19. י"ד א"ח　[3] Exod. xviii : 21. ח"א, ד"י, ח"מ　[4] Jeremiah xxix : 5. Lev. xxii : 31. ח"מ,י"ד

all their hearts, with all their souls, and all their might. Thus will you be individually and in your restricted circle what it is the mission of your people to be everywhere and forever.

THIRTEENTH LETTER.

Edoth. — *Symbolic Observances.* — The acknowledgment of the essential principles of life in righteousness and love does not suffice to actually build up such a life, nor is it even sufficient for the accomplishment of your mission as Israelite, as bearer of the law of God to man, actually to live in accordance with those fundamental principles; there is need, in addition thereto, of symbolic words and actions which shall stamp them indelibly upon the soul, and thus preserve them for you and for others. A truth, in order to produce results, must be impressed upon the mind and heart repeatedly and emphatically. This is the essential concept of the Edoth. The symbols are chiefly those of actions, of practices which serve as signs of an idea. Thus the doctrine that God is the creator and possessor of all; that all is His; man the admin-

trator according to His will, and Israel the
teacher of the law of humanity's mission, is
symbolized in the commandments בכור, the
sanctity of the first-born, חלה, the giving of
the portion of dough, ערלה, the prohibition of
the use of immature fruit, חרש, the prohibition of the use of the new grain previous to
the offering of the measure of barley, שבת, the
Sabbath, and in reference to Israel's holy soil
through the Sabbatical and Jubilee years,
תרומה ויובל שמטה, the heave-offering and
בכורים, the offering of the first ripe fruits.

The doctrine that God is the Redeemer and
Savior of Israel, and also He that revealed
His holy law to His chosen nation, is symbolized by פסח, the Passover festival, שבועות,
the Feast of Weeks, סכות, the Feast of
Tabernacles and שמיני עצרת, the Eighth
day of Solemn Assembly. That God is to us
in exile what He was to our ancestors, is symbolized in חנוכה, Hanuccah, the Memorial of
the Re-dedication of the Temple and in פורים,
Purim, the Memorial of the deliverance from
Haman. Acknowledgment that the *spirit*

vivifies the body and that law is needful as a
regulation to freedom is symbolized 'in the
ספירה, the counting of the days between
Passover and the Feast of Weeks.   Consideration of the causes of the exile and
warning to shun the sins which have led
thereto are inculcated by the תעניות, fast
days.   To keep even the body and its organs
pure and holy, and to shun all that leads to
bestiality is taught by מילה, circumcision.
To dedicate all the powers of our mind,
heart, and body to the service of the All-One
is the lesson of תפלין, the Phylacteries. Reminder of the presence of the Invincible One
and of His revelation in the past, limitation
and repression of sensuality as a weapon for
battle against evil, are the purposes of ציצת,
the show-threads.   Consecration of the Jewish
home as a temple of God, of the Jewish life
therein as a perpetual service of God, is the
aim of מזוזה, the sacred inscription on the door
posts. Recognition of the Jacob-state in Israel,
that is, of the lack of external might and in-
dependence as a requirement of a truly

spiritual conception of the Israel-mission to
teach the revelation of God, is symbolized in
the מצה, bread of afflicton, and גיד הנשה,
prohibition of the sinew of the hip that was
lamed.

A wise appreciation and use of property,
equally removed from the two extremes of
scorn and over-estimation, is taught by לולב,
the palm-branch of the Succoth festival, and
by סוכה, the symbolic booth. As concerns
the land of Israel, the same lesson is taught
by מעשרות, the tithe-offering. Finally, that
highest and most solemn thought known to
religion, that God is the supreme Ruler,
Judge, and Father; that it is our duty to
scrutinize our doings in life in order to know
whether they really come up to the high demands of the Holy Law; that it is our duty,
when necessary, to recognize and confess our
short-comings, which have deprived us of our
claim to life, and made us dependent for existence and preservation solely upon the Divine
mercy, and that it is incumbent upon us to
strive to lift ourselves up to a higher plane and

a purer future ; these sublime and holy truths are taught by ר"ה וי"כ, the New Year and Atonement-day, by שופר ור"ח, by the solemn blast of the ram's-horn, by the rites of the New Month.[1] These symbolic acts and seasons all give expression to ideas, without splitting them up into words as speech must. They come to the mind each a unit, like thought itself, and like the resolve which they should beget; they present themselves with all the force of a single, undivided, and indi-

---

[1] In giving this sketchy and superficial account of the *Mitzvoth* (Commandments), and particularly in regard to the *Edoth* and *Abodah* (symbolic practices and worship), I must presuppose that the Mitzvoth are, in general, known to you from your study of Bible and Talmud, or from their practical exemplification in life. It is not my purpose to describe the Mitzvoth themselves. You will find difficulty in harmonizing some of them with the concepts given here. My intention is only to state the concepts under which I arrange them in my mind, merely as a sort of inscription upon the receptacles, in which they are contained, in order to arouse in you the desire to become more thoroughly acquainted with their contents, and also to give you data to settle for yourself the question, "Is this really the concept of the Mitzvoth?"

To *demonstrate* that this and many other theories of mine are really correct and true, I reserve, as I have already frequently mentioned, for a future work.

visible appeal to the soul. Therefore they are appropriate vehicles to convey the sentiments of a single united nation pervaded with one thought, actuated by one resolve, and are intelligible beyond the confines of Israelitish nationality. Every single detail of action or omission in the *Edoth*-division of the Law is a writing, a word, a speech addressed to the reverent devotee; they are, all of them, reminders to the soul or vivid expressions of sentiment by means of significant action-language. The greatest and the least of them, even the never-enough-to-be-ridiculed prohibition of the use of an egg laid on Sabbath or holiday, symbolically teach a lesson, and the strict attention paid to so-called trifles is not more worthy of ridicule and not less sensible than your care to use a clear and intelligible language or a legible and neat handwriting. Let us take, for instance, the law of Sabbath, with its prohibition of labor. Many of the minor details of what our Sages technically call מלאכה, "labor," we would hardly recognize as such, and yet not even the pettiest and most insignificant thereof but has its reason and definite purpose.

The day upon which the newly-created world first lay extended in its completeness before man that he might possess and rule over it, this day was to be to him an eternal monument of the great truth that all around him was the possession of God, the Creator, and that God it was who had conferred upon him the power and the right to rule it, in order that he should not grow overweening in his dominion and should administer his trust as the property of God and in accordance with His supreme will.   In order to retain this idea ever fresh and vivid, he should refrain on this day from exercising his human sway over the things of earth, should not place his hand upon any object for the purpose of human dominion, that is, to employ it for any human end; he must, as it were, return the borrowed world to its Divine Owner in order to realize that it is but lent to him.   On this account the labor forbidden on the Sabbath is chiefly מלאכת מחשבת, that is to say, *productive* ac-

tivity, executed consciously, with purpose and
proper means, in order to produce a certain result, an action, therefore, which is the outcome
of human will and conscious force, not, however, קלקול, "an action which produces no
desired result," מתעסק, "purposeless occupation," שאינו מתכון, "unintentional work,"
שאינה צריכה לגופה, "in itself unnecessary,"
כלאחר יד, "indirectly performed," or not
in שעור, "proper measure and proportion."
Do you not see that every moment of the
Sabbath that you restrain your hand from
labor you proclaim God the only Creator
and Master and yourself as his servant? Do
you not see that even the slightest, least ardu-
ous, productive action on the Sabbath in-
volves the denial of God as Creator and Lord,
and the usurpation on your part of the throne
of God? The desecration of the Sabbath is
therefore equivalent to the entire rejection and
negation of the Israel-mission. Do you not
recognize that the Sabbath is not a mere day
of physical recuperation, but that it is ברית,
"a covenant," זכרון, "a sacred memorial,"

אות, "a profoundly instructive sign?" It is
קודש, a sacred day which is not instituted
solely that man may rest after the labors of
the week which is past, but may consecrate
himself to the tasks of the week which is to
come.

The Sabbath is thus an institution of vast
significance, but not it alone, every one of the
many ordinances which constitute the *Edoth*
is similarly laden with great and invaluable instruction, and both those ordinances deducible
from the plain word of Scripture, דאורייתא,
and those established by Rabbinical interpretation, דרבנן, are equally instructive and important.

FOURTEENTH LETTER.

The last division of the Holy Law, Abodah (service or worship), remains for our consideration.

Abodah, the service of God; it means to turn away from the ambitions, the occupations, and the sins which mainly constitute our material existence, and to strive to regain the eternal verities of the higher life when they have gone astray from us in the deceptions, errors, conflicts, and temptations of the world. עבודה שבלב, heart service, our Sages love to call true devotion; that is, to fulfill the will of God towards our inner parts by purifying and ennobling our unseen power, our character.

תפלה, prayer, is our chief form of serving the Supreme One in the present age, but the Hebrew conception of prayer is not the mere request or petition for Divine aid, nor even a mere ecstasy of devotion and adoration; it

means the possession and expression of proper
conceptions and resolutions concerning our
own personality and our duties toward God,
the world, and mankind.   In former days the
sacrificial rite was the expression of our service of God; its ordinances and ceremonies
were symbolic actions of profound significance.
The Temple, the dwelling of the Torah, itself
Israel's most sacred possession, taught the
lesson that the Law was God's gift to Israel
(ארון), and that for its fulfillment God had
given unto man the power of body and mind.
(שלחן and מנורה.)   The sacrifices, each in-
culcates its individual meaning, the suppression of sensuality,[1] of selfishness,[2] the consecration of life,[3] of the sentiments,[4] of one's
entire personality,[5] to God for the fulfillment
of his Law.   Some of them typify the endeavor to consecrate oneself to God through
the Torah,[6] others the effort to regain lost
purity of life by the suppression of sensuality
and selfishness, equivalent to return to the

---

[1] קטורת   [2] זריקת דם־דם   [3] הקטרת חלב   [4] הקטרת כבד and כליות
[5] עולה   [6] עולה

Law;[1] others, again, the recognition of God
as the Giver of the great good things of life
or the Preserver of our peace and happiness.[2] This recognition of the Divine be-
nevolence must be complete, sincere, and
free from every material and sensual thought.
Our gratitude must be extended to Him because He has given us so much which we
can consecrate to the fulfillment of His holy
will as revealed in the Torah. These symbolic actions were all accompanied by the
living word of fervent devotion. (See Maimonides הלכות תמידים, Chap. vi.) The
temple is sunk into ruins, but the living
word of worship and instruction remains, com-
pleter even than in former times, because the
symbolic rites of sacrifices must be represented
also by it. The aim of our worship, תפלה
from התפלל, is the purification, enlightenment, and uplifting of our inner selves to the
recognition of the Most High and our duties
towards Him in truth; not mere stirring up
of the emotions, swiftly-vanishing devotion,

---

[1] תורה and שלמים   [2] חטאת and אשם

empty sentimentalism, and unreasoning tears,
but the cleansing of thought and heart.

Life robs us of the correct judgment concerning God, the world, man, and Israel, and
concerning our own relation to them. Leaving
the disturbing influences of life and turning
to God, you can approach and find Him in the
mystic contemplations of the Tefillah. All
the various component parts of the Hebrew
worship subserve this great purpose, the bringing of man into communication with Him
who is concealed from view in his (man's)
daily life. תהלות, the psalms or praises; they
show us ecstatic visions of God in nature, the
world of man and in Israel. תפלות, the
prayers or devotions; they stir up our nature
to its deepest depths and lift us up to com-
munion with the Divine. תודות, thanks-
givings and בקשות, supplications ; they express our profound gratitude for all that Deity
has wrought and our full and unrestricted acknowledgment that everything past or future
proceeds from His hands, and our humble
petition that He may continue His bounty

unto us, though we be unworthy. תחנות,
humble appeals to His unfailing mercy to heal
our weaknesses and backslidings. The scientific foundation and basis upon which all this
edifice of worship is raised is the קריאת
התורה, "reading of the Law," which im-
parts unto us the instruction and wisdom
which we require; its utmost summit and
goal, the perfect fruit of our piety, are the
ברכות, benedictions, which supply us the firm
resolution actively to promote the fulfillment
of the Divine will in the midst of life, so
busy with transitory cares and devoted pre-
eminently to material aims. Retain these
sketchy outlines in your mind, and bearing
them in memory contemplate afresh our
prayers, our service as a whole, and see if
you do not find it more dignified, fuller of
meaning and importance than you had ever
before imagined.

"*Shools*," that is, schools, we call our
houses of worship, and that is what they
should be, schools for the grown-up, for
those who have long since exchanged the

tasks of the schoolmaster for the problems
of life.

And now, my dear Benjamin, a law which
bids us recognize God in the world and in
mankind, which teaches that the fulfillment of
His will is our mission, which shows us in
Him the Father of all beings, of all men and
in every creature, every human being our
brother; a law which makes our whole life
service of God through the practice of righteousness and love toward all beings and the
proclaiming of these truths for ourselves and
others; can this be a law which stunts the
mind and the heart, limits every joy of life
and turns men into secluded monks? Can it
be that the study of this law, when pursued
earnestly and intelligently, perverts and
deadens the mind, narrows or restricts the impulses of the heart?

Its true description is found in the words of
the sweet singer of Israel:
" The heavens declare themselves
Revelation of God's glory;
The thin sheet of space (declares)

That it is His handiwork.
Day proclaims to day
That God has spoken;
Night after night revives
The thoughts of Deity.
No speech we need,
No words are spoken,
Without them the voice is heard.
Through all the earth their voice goes forth,
To the end of the earth-world their words.
In them He hath set the tent of the sun,
Which it leaves as a bridegroom his canopy;
It rejoices, as the Almighty, to run its course.
And yet fixed in heaven is its issue,
Its circuit reaches ever the same end,
None are hidden from his sun.
But only the law of God is complete,
Giving answer to th' inquiring soul;
The testimony of God alone is faithful,
Giving wisdom to th' unlearned;
Th' ordinances of God are righteous,
Giving joy to the heart;
The commands of God are clear,
Giving light to the eyes;

The fear of God is pure,
Existing forever;
The judgments of God are true,
They are right altogether,
Better than gold and much ore,
Sweeter than honey and dripping comb.
O, that Thy servant might be illumed by them!
To keep them is the great path of life."
    (Ps. xix.)

FIFTEENTH LETTER.

You tell me, my dear Benjamin, that you have taken as your device the utterance of the Psalmist, "O, that Thy servant might be illumed by them, to keep them is the great path of life;" that you have vowed to know no rest until you have gained this inner light; to establish not your house until you have added to your rich store of external goods the internal treasures of the Torah, in order that you may be able to use your possessions worthily and in accordance with the will of God, and in order that your house be established in the Torah-spirit for Israel—humanity.

These words are to me proof and guarantee that I have not written in vain.

Do come to me in accordance with your resolution; you have my most cordial invitation, and I shall endeavor to explain to you verbally and in detail what you now have become acquainted with in mere sketchy outlines. Do

135

not expect, however, to find in me an infallible master. I shall confess to you honestly whenever I myself am in doubt and darkness, and shall endeavor to incite you thus to independent research. You wish me to spare myself the trouble of refuting your first letter; you have examined it thoroughly in the light of your new knowledge and answered it yourself. I am, indeed, overjoyed that you have done so. I have, however, already prepared my answer, although only in the first rough cast. I send it to you so that you may compare it with your own thoughts; you need expect nothing more than fragments of thoughts. It was but natural that you found Judaism in contradiction to your conception of the purpose of human existence, inasmuch as your conception was one which Judaism rejects, and against whose lower elements, desire of pleasure and deification of material possessions, it wages unceasing warfare.

These lower potencies in the materialistic view of the world are somewhat refined and spiritualized by the higher professors of that system, but are not essentially altered or abrogated. The essential notion of this system is either that of the world without an active God or of God without a world that serves Him. Judaism takes another and a higher view, and predicates even the highest and best as means only to that higher end. Doubtless you now comprehend our national misfortunes as the product of our national shortcomings, shortcomings which do not, by any means, however, lower us in point of righteousness below the standard of the other nations. Israel never committed a sin which the other nations of the world did not also commit. But the standard applied to Israel was a higher one; what Deity readily pardons to others He would not forgive to us; the destruction of the Israel-state, which had fallen short of its high ideals, was the direct consequence of these universal sins; it was a part of the Divine administration of Israel's career.

"And God punished in him the sin of us all."

Israel's material weakness and deprivation

of worldly joys and glory seem to you now a part of the scheme of its God-revealing existence; you realize that the external humility of the nation's lot did not disturb its mission nor diminish its greatness. It simply exchanged one kind of greatness for another, and in dispersion there was opened to it a new and broader field for the fulfillment of its mission.

And as for the Law, is it really a preventative of all the joys of life, a hindrance and an obstacle to the gratification of the natural human craving for pleasure? Examine once the precepts and ordinances of the Law from beginning to end and tell me what legitimate desire it forbids to gratify, what natural impulse it would destroy or extirpate.

On the contrary, it purifies and sanctifies even our lower impulses and desires by applying them with wise limitation to the purposes designated by the Creator.

Righteousness is the Law's typical end and aim, the gratification of physical lust and passion is never its object. Therefore are the

lower cravings subordinated to higher law
and limited by the Creator's wisdom for His
infinitely wise purposes; but as means of
attaining proper and necessary ends, the Law
recognizes these desires as perfectly moral,
pure, and human, and their carrying out as
just and as legitimate as the fulfillment of
any other human task or mission.

What the Law, however, firmly and un-
yieldingly opposes is the deification of wealth
and lust as the sole aim and controlling impulse of our lives; but it not only permits
their pursuit within the limits set by Divine
wisdom, but declares the effort to gain them a
duty as sacred and binding as any other
human obligation, and condemns the purposeless and unreasonable abstinence from permitted indulgences as sin.[1] How could the
reverse of this be possible? Is it conceivable
that God would bestow upon man any power
or capacity and then, by utter prohibition of
its use, legally annihilate it? Highest and
truest worship is it to be "joyous before the

---

[1] תענית י״א and כ״ב

Lord;'' to pass one's life in gladsome lightness of spirit because of the consciousness
that we live under the eye of God and that
His protecting hand is ever outstretched to
guide and guard us in every danger and trial;
to think and feel, to speak and work, to enjoy
and to endure. Then, through a higher comprehension of them both, shall we be reconciled
to suffering and happiness alike, realizing that
all our varied experiences belong to our task,
and that our only eternal purpose in life is
joyously to solve its problems.

Has this people furnished no contribution
to the great edifice of human civilization? I
shall not ask whether any of the other peoples ever consciously did anything with a view
to the furtherance of universal human happiness. I shall not ask whether they did not
all seek only their own welfare, nor whether
they ever performed any deed of general value
except unconsciously, as blind instruments in
the hand of God; neither shall I inquire
whether all was indeed productive of blessing,
but I shall, indeed, challenge the world to

deny that Israel, consciously, and at the sacrifice of its earthly peace and well-being, saved
as a palladium from the shipwreck of its fortunes the only thing through which science,
culture, art, and inventive skill could become
the means of bringing true blessing and salvation to the world. Is there any truer greatness for men than to be the bearers of revealed
instruction concerning God and the duty of
man, and to show by example and life that
there are higher things than wealth and
pleasure, than science and culture, to which
these should be but subordinate means of fulfillment?

Does not this law erect a wall of separation
between its adherents and the rest of mankind? It does, I admit, but had it not done
so Israel would long since have lost all consciousness of its mission, would long since have
ceased to be itself. Do you not perceive what
struggles the preservation of the true Israel-
spirit in our midst requires, despite this separation? How, then, could the holy flame have
been kept burning in our breasts had there

been no distinctive laws and ordinances to re-
mind us that we are consecrated to a sacred
duty, a Divine mission? But whosoever *honestly*
thinks that our isolation is the result of pride
or of hostility to our fellow beings is the vic-
tim of a deplorable delusion.   Is not God the
loving Father of all creatures, of all human
beings ?

Has Israel any other task than to teach all
the races of man to recognize and worship
the Only-One as their God ? Is it not Israel's
unceasing duty to proclaim through the example of its life and history Him as the Universal Lord and Sovereign ?   The Bible terms
Israel סגלה, "a peculiar treasure," but this
designation does not imply, as some have
falsely interpreted, that Israel has a monopoly
of the Divine love and favor, but, on the contrary, that God has the sole and exclusive
claim to Israel's devotions and service; that
Israel may not render Divine homage to any
other being.[1]   Israel's most cherished ideal

---

[1] סגלה means a property belonging exclusively to one owner,
to which no other has any right or claim. Compare ב"פ ס"ז

is that of the universal brotherhood of mankind.   Almost every page of the prayers we
utter contains supplication for the hastening
of this consummation.   We are all helping to
rear a great edifice, Divinely ordained for the
well-being of man; all nations that were or
are anywhere upon the surface of the earth,
whether in the east or the west, the north or
the south, each with its life and its disappear-
ance from the stage of history, with its suc-
cesses and its failures, with its virtues and its
vices, its wisdom and its folly, its rise and its
fall, in a word, with whatsoever it leaves to
posterity as the sum total of the results and
products of its existence.

All of these efforts and actions are bricks
contributed to the edifice of human history;
all tend to the carrying out of the plan of the
one, same God.[1]

This is the lesson of the life of all the good
and virtuous of all nations, of whosoever

[1] חסידי א״ה יש להם חלק להם לעולם הבא is a saying of the
sages which may be interpreted as meaning that all nations
will help to work out the historical destiny of humanity.

gave the example of unselfish righteousness and the true dignity of humanity; this is what has been striven for by all whose souls have been illumed by light from on high and who, by word or deed, have helped to lift their brethren up to the All-One, to diffuse respect for justice and to elevate man above the beast; the same result is attained by the art of the Greeks when morally pure and devoted to the refinement of the mind, and of their science, when sharpening the intellect to the better apprehension of truth; even the sword of the Roman and the peaceful commerce of the European have united nations in brotherhood for the working out of the same ideals:—and Israel has done and will do its share of the glorious task.

Is not the spirit prostrated and degraded by the absolute devotion which this law requires, so that the observant Jew loses the courage and the strength which free contact with the world and participation in its affairs give? The question is a familiar one and often put, but I ask you, "Whom do you respect more, who is really the stronger, the downtrodden Jew, who possesses in the dust of humility sufficient strength of mind and character to pity his opponent and to accept the scorn heaped upon him as a trial sent by God and as a part of the destiny of his nation, or the ruffian, who, in his overweening pride, abuses the weakness of his fellow man, seems to consider himself privileged to revile the feeble and impotent and to find therein his claim to greatness?''

Do not say that this conception of God, the world, and humanity clogs the progress of science, and as for art, the plastic arts, why, since men began to forget the All-One and to deify His creatures, even to worship their own animal impulses, whose omnipotence they felt, and to glorify them in symbols of stone, so that every god statue became a sad memento of human degradation; since then, truly, Judaism interdicts the making and possession of such images, for to it truth is higher and greater than art. Certainly, no artist inspired with the true spirit of Judaism would

take the chisel, the brush, or the pencil in his
hand to form an art-work adapted only to stir
up impure imaginations and to rouse the
animal in man; for, if such productions of art
be deemed useful and proper, then are morality
and virtue mere empty words and not, as we
conceive them to be, in reality the standard
and the measure of our actions.

You speak of dogmas, dogmas of faith ! In
answer thereto, I would briefly say that Judaism enjoins six hundred and thirteen duties,
but knows no dogmas. The sublime truths
which lie at its basis, it reveals as axioms,
clearly intelligible to all who have ears to hear
and minds to comprehend, and in this way
opens a field for the broadest investigation and
profoundest research into the essence and relations of all things to each other; it rouses us
to the endeavor to understand the world, man,
human history, and God's plan operating
therein. In this effort personal study and
thought, universal human experience and the
Torah are to be alike utilized, for the latter is
as real and actual a source of instruction as

the two former. True speculation does not consist, as many would-be thinkers suppose, in closing the eye and the ear to the world round about us and in constructing out of our own inner Ego a world to suit ourselves; true speculation takes nature, man, and history as facts, as the true basis of knowledge, and seeks in them instruction and wisdom; to these Judaism adds the Torah, as genuine a reality as heaven or earth. But it regards no speculation which does not lead to active, productive life as its ultimate goal; it points out the limits of our understanding and warns us against baseless reasoning, transcending the legitimate bounds of our intellectual capacity, however brilliantly put together and glitteringly logical it may appear to be, for all such intellectual pyrotechnics are, after all, but puerile sport, useful chiefly to still the conscientious scruples of a sensual nature, oblivious alike to the limitations and the ideals of humanity. To be sure, the Jewish spirit, in its most recent form, was chiefly devoted to abstract and abstruse speculation; a vivid con-

sciousness of the real world was lacking, and
therefore the object of study was not what it
should chiefly have been, the attainment of
knowledge of duty, for use in the world and
in life. Study became the end instead of the
means, the subject of investigation became a
matter of indifference, the dialectic subtleties
thereof the chief concern; people studied
Judaism but forgot to search for its principles
in the pages of Scripture. That method is,
however, not truly Jewish; our great masters
have always protested against it; many pages
of the classic works of Jewish literature are
filled with the objections of their authors to
this false and perverted method. Bible and
Talmud are to be studied with one sole object
in view, to ascertain the life-duties which they
inculcate, ללמוד וללמד לשמור ולעשות, "to
learn and to teach—to observe and to do,"
and every topic treated of in the Law should
be viewed objectively or a comprehension
thereof obtained from science. There is no
science which trains the mind to a broader
and more practical view of things than does

the Torah, pursued in this manner. That the Law, which lays down Reverence, Love, and Faithfulness as its three foundation-stones, does not cripple the heart, but that, when comprehended and assimilated to the mind, its fulfillment becomes a new power, a life from within, not a mere barren and external dwarf of existence, stimulating all the faculties to a freer development and a more intense use—you have already demonstrated by your adhesion.

"Chasid," pious one! a glorious name, but misunderstood and deformed through ignorant or malicious misconception coming from without; the true חסיד is he who devotes himself in love entirely to the service of the Higher Power, who does not seek for himself aught, but relinquishes his claims upon the world in order that he may live more actively and carry out more thoroughly works of love for the world; he does not withdraw from its midst, but lives in it, with it, and for it. The Chasid is for himself, nothing; for the world, everything. David, therefore, who labored

from his earliest youth continuously and exclusively for the internal and external well-
being of his people, and who left the repara-
tion of the injury done him by Saul and the
disposal of his own affairs to the wisdom of
Deity alone; he, indeed, deserves to be called
חסיד. You know the Rabbinical definition
of the term "‏שלך שלך ושלי שלך חסיד‎."
He who says, "That which is thine is thine
and mine is also thine, is a Chasid," but a
life of seclusion devoted only to meditation
and prayer is not Judaism. Study and worship are but paths which lead to work, תלמור
‏גדול שמביא לידי מעשה‎. "Great is
study, for it leads to practical fulfillment of
the precepts," is a saying of our sages, and
the flower and fruit of our devotions should
be the resolve to lead a life of activity, pervaded with the spirit of God. Such a life
is the only and universal goal.

As for the causes which produced these
errors in the theory and practice of life, we
shall speak of them, perhaps, on some later
occasion.

But how about the difficulty of obeying this law in our time—the trouble which it causes while travelling, in intercourse with Gentiles, and in business? I will admit, for the sake of argument, that all the complaints which the children of the age give utterance to concerning the difficulty and trouble of obeying the Jewish law are true. If our view of life is earnest and serious; if we comprehend Judaism as the charge with which we are entrusted, and which we are to bear through time and tribulation; if we realize that it is our life-code of duty, can the difficulty, the burdensomeness of an obligation dispense us from its fulfillment? Should it not rather make the duty of fulfillment more solemn and urgent?

But let us examine the alleged difficulties more closely—from the standpoint of the spirit of Judaism—and they will disappear altogether. We will take up your last first—business.

O! son of age, do you really think that you cannot fulfill the Law because it commands

your business to cease during one-seventh of
your time, in order that you should thereby
manifest your conviction that in God is the
source of your strength and your right to the
possession of the world; that from Him comes
the blessing, and in order that you may consecrate yourself and make yourself worthy to
use His blessings as sacred, Divine gifts according to His desire; do you really deem
yourself unable to obey the Law, because it
asks you to reserve another seventeenth of
your time, not for the ordinary tasks of daily
existence, but to lead your thoughts again to
your mission as an Israelite, and to strengthen
you to fulfill properly your nation's allotted
task on earth?

Son of the present! do you not blush to
utter such a complaint? Certainly, if you
consider yourself born only to possess and to
enjoy; if the quantity and extent of your possessions and enjoyments are for you the measure of your importance; if you look upon
these things, not as a means, but as ends in
themselves; if you think that your business

activity is essentially different from that of the
agriculturist, who can do no more than to
place the seed in the earth, but must look to
the blessing of God's sun and God's rain to
ripen and develop it; if you believe that your
strength and the power of your hand can carry
the edifice of your prosperity to its summit;
not God, but you alone, and that all other
considerations must yield to this one ambition,
then—then, indeed —— —— !

Not so is the spirit of Judaism! If you
would comprehend the Sabbath and its beautiful, ideal lessons; if you would realize that in
and through it are given to you at once the
basis of your earthly task, and its sublimest,
most spiritual fulfillment; that it proclaims
you a witness that a God, that *one* God is, and
that man is created for His service; if, on the
other hand, you would thoroughly reflect on
all the insane monstrousness of the thought,
"for the sake of gain to desecrate the Sabbath;" in order to gain my daily bread or to
increase my wealth, that I may possess the
means better to fulfill my duties to God, I

deny that there is a God to whom belongs the
world and the fullness thereof; I deny that
from Him come life and its blessings, I affirm
that wealth and the gratification of desire are
my only purpose, fulfillment of my will my
only object; I negate both God and the mission
of humanity; . . . surely, these reflections
should cause you to let fall again the hand
which lust for gain had raised to desecrate
the Sabbath.   Yes, if you would but contemplate your life in the spirit of the Sabbath,
if you would for but one single moment comprehend yourself as viewed by the eternal
gaze of God, as the Sabbath teaches that you
are; if you would comprehend yourself as viv-
ified of God, in a God-filled world, the totality
of its life directed by God; if you would feel
yourself child and servant of the All-One; all
your existence dependent upon the will of the
All-Only Father and Lord, every breath His
gift, every faculty His offering, every event in
your history His doing; you, His servant,
your whole life fulfillment of His commandments ; — would you then still comprehend

your present complaint? You would then comprehend that your longing to possess is but one of your duties, and essentially the same as any of the others, and esteem your possessions, not according to the amount of the property you have acquired, but according to the degree of compliance with the Divine commandments you have observed in accumulating it, as well as in using and applying it; you would understand that though the six days bring you the external means of fulfilling your mission, the seventh alone can afford you the inner means, spiritual power and consecration, and that these blessed results can only be attained if both gain and disposal be in accordance with the Divine precept; you would see that since God it is who has given you power to earn and blessing in the accumulation, He is also rich and strong enough to shower upon your dwelling so much manna in six days that on the seventh you would not lack, then you would feel that you do not, because of that complaint, cease to be a Jew, but that you must have ceased to be a Jew, in the only true and real sense, before you could utter such a complaint. "But how about intercourse with non-Jews? One makes oneself so conspicuous, is recognized at once as a Jew!" Son of the present, who tells you to deny or conceal the fact that you are a Jew? Be a Jew; be it really and truly; endeavor to attain to the ideal of the true Jew in fulfillment of the law of justice, righteousness, and love, then will you be respected, not in spite of the fact that you are a Jew, but because of it; comprehend yourself as Jew, and disseminate that comprehension by word and deed among your non-Jewish brethren, and you will have no occasion to complain that your Judaism cannot travel incognito. "But one cannot become truly intimate, truly sociable, if one does not, at least, eat and drink with them at their banquets!") Again, I would say, practise righteousness and love as the Holy Law bids you; be just in deed, truthful in word, bear love in your heart for your non-Jewish brethren, as your Law teaches you; feed his hungry, clothe his naked, console his mourners, heal his sick.

counsel his inexperienced, assist him with counsel and deed in need and sorrow, unfold the whole noble breadth of your Israeldom, and can you think that he will not respect and love you, or that there will not result as great a degree of social intimacy as your life can concede?

But you would have more; the right to enter into his family as a member thereof! Do you not see that, until the advent of the age of universal brotherhood, you should not, cannot, desire that? Not, however, on account of enmity or hostility, but because of your Israel-mission. You cannot be angry with the Law, if it interdicts for you marriage alliance outside of Israel, because you should rear your children, the most precious pledges of the Divine love, only for His Torah, and it would mean to lead them away from the Torah, if you would not be to them an Israel-itish father, or would give them other than an Israelitish mother. You must be grateful, therefore, to the Law that it seeks to prevent the sons of Israel from amorous attachment to non-Israelitish daughters or non-Israelitish sons to the daughters of Israel.

Comprehend the object of your life, comprehend the Israel-duty, and there will disappear as a thin mist all the alleged difficulty of upholding Judaism, felt so keenly in our time only because the Israel-spirit has vanished, or because Israel's sons know not nor respect themselves; because they even, in part, demand the violation of the Israel-duty.

SIXTEENTH LETTER.

You ask me for my opinion on the question which at present agitates so greatly the minds of men, emancipation; whether I consider it feasible and desirable, according to the spirit of Judaism, our duty to strive to attain it. The new conception of Judaism which you have gained, dear Benjamin, has rendered you uncertain as to the reconcilability of Gentile citizenship with the eternal ideals of our faith. You have begun to doubt whether the acceptance of these new relations be in harmony with the spirit of Judaism, inasmuch as it approximates to a close union with that which is different and alien, and a severance of the ties

---

[1] This letter is explained through the circumstance that at the time of its composition the emancipation of the Jews was not yet an accomplished fact in most European states, though everywhere proposed and discussed. It is remarkable with what accuracy Hirsch comprehended the nature of his brethren and how literally his apprehensions of a misunderstanding of the purpose of emancipation by a great section of the Jewish people have been fulfilled. (The Translator.)

which bind us to the Israel lot; you doubt its
desirability, because through over much intimacy with the Gentile, Israel's peculiar
characteristics could easily be obliterated. I
respect your scruples, and will communicate
to you my own opinion. Let us first examine
whether it be in harmony with the spirit of
Judaism.

When Israel began its great wandering
through the ages and nations, Jeremiah proclaimed the following as its duty:

"Build houses and dwell therein;[1] plant
gardens and eat the fruit thereof; take wives
unto yourselves, and beget sons and daughters,
and take wives for your sons and give your
daughters in marriage that they bear sons and
daughters, and that you multiply there and
diminish not. And seek the peace of the city
whither I have exiled you, and pray for it to
the Lord, for in its peace there will be unto
you peace."

To be pushed back and limited upon the
path of life is, therefore, not an essential con-

---

[1] Jeremiah xvix :5 ₹.

dition of the Galuth, Israel's exile state among
the nations, but, on the contrary, it is our
duty to join ourselves as closely as possible to
the state which receives us into its midst, to
promote its welfare and not to consider our
well-being as in any way separate from that
of the state to which we belong.

This close connection with all states is
in nowise in contradiction to the spirit of
Judaism, for the former independent state life
of Israel was not even then the essence or purpose of our national existence, was only a
means of fulfilling our spiritual mission.

Land and soil were never Israel's bond of
union, but only the common task of the Torah;
therefore, it still forms a united body, though
separated from a national soil; nor does this
unity lose its reality, though Israel accept
everywhere the citizenship of the nations
amongst which it is dispersed. This coherence of sympathy, this spiritual union,
which may be designated by the Hebrew
terms עם and גוי, but not by the expression " nation," unless we are able to separate

from the term the concept of common terri-
tory and political power, is the only communal band we possess, or ever expect to
possess, until the great day shall arrive when
the Almighty shall see fit, in His inscrutable
wisdom, to unite again His scattered servants
in one land, and the Torah shall be the guiding principle of a state, an exemplar of the
meaning of Divine Revelation and the mission
of humanity.

For this future, which is promised us in the
glorious predictions of the inspired prophets,
whom God raised up for our ancestors, we
hope and pray; but actively to accelerate its
coming were sin, and is prohibited to us, while
the entire purpose of the Messianic age is that
we may, in prosperity, exhibit to mankind a
better example of "Israel" than did our
ancestors the first time, while, hand in hand
with us, the entire race will be joined in universal brotherhood through the recognition of
God, the All-One.

On account of this purely spiritual nature
of the national character of Israel it is capable

of the most intimate union with states, with, perhaps, this difference, that while others seek in the state only the material benefits which it secures, considering possession and enjoyment as the highest good, Israel can only regard it as a means of fulfilling the mission of humanity.

Summon up, I pray you, before your mental vision, the picture of such an Israel, dwelling in freedom in the midst of the nations, and striving to attain unto its ideal, every son of Israel a respected and influential exemplar priest of righteousness and love, disseminating among the nations not specific Judaism, for proselytism is interdicted, but pure humanity. What a mighty impulse to progress, what a luminary and staff in the gloomy days of the Middle Ages had not Israel's sin and the insanity of the nations rendered such a *Galuth* impossible! How impressive, how sublime it would have been, if, in the midst of a race that adored only power, possessions, and enjoyment, and that was oft blinded by superstitious imaginings, there had lived quietly and publicly human beings of a different sort, who beheld in material possessions only the means of practising justice and love towards all; whose minds, pervaded with the wisdom and truth of the law, maintained simple, straightforward views, and emphasized them for themselves and others in expressive, vivid deed-symbols.

But it would seem as though Israel was to be fitted through the endurance of harsh and cruel exile for the proper appreciation and utilization of its milder and gentler form.

When *Galuth* will be comprehended and accepted as it should be, when in suffering, the service of God and His Torah will be understood as the only task of life, when even in misery God will be served, and external abundance esteemed only as a means of this service, then, perhaps, Israel will be ready for the greater temptations of prosperity and happiness in dispersion. Just as it is our duty to endeavor to obtain those material possessions which are the fundamental condition of life, so also is it the duty of every one to take advantage of every alleviation and improve-

ment of his condition open to him in a righteous way; for, the more means, the more
opportunity is given to him to fulfill his mission in its broadest sense; and no less than of
the individual is it the duty of the community
to obtain for all its members the opportunities
and privileges of citizenship and liberty. Do
I consider it desirable? I bless emancipation,
when I see how the excess of oppression drove
Israel away from human intercourse, prevented
the cultivation of the mind, limited the free
development of the noble sides of character,
and compelled many individuals to enter, for
the sake of self-support, upon paths which,
to be sure men filled with the true spirit of
Judaism would have shunned even in the
extremest necessity, but the temptation to
enter upon which they were too weak to with-
stand.

I bless emancipation when I notice that no
spiritual principle, even such as are born of
superstitious self-deception, stands in its way,
but only those passions degrading to humanity,
lust for gain and narrow selfishness; I rejoice

when I perceive that in this concession of emancipation, regard for the inborn rights of men to live as equals among equals, and the principle that whosoever bears the seal of a child of God, unto whom belongs the earth, shall be willingly acknowledged by all as brother, are freely acknowledged without force or compulsion, but purely through the power of their inner truth and demand, as a natural consequence, the sacrifice of the base passions, love of self and gain. I welcome this sacrifice, wherever it is offered, as the dawn of reviving humanity in mankind, as a preliminary step to the universal recognition of God as the only Lord and Father, of all human beings as the children of the All-One, and consequently brethren, and of the earth as soil common to all, and bestowed upon them by God to be administered in accordance with His will. But for Israel I only bless it if at the same time there awakes in Israel the true spirit, which, independent of emancipation or non-emancipation, strives to fulfill the Israel-mission: to elevate and ennoble ourselves, to

implant the spirit of Judaism in our souls, in
order that it may produce a life in which that
spirit shall be reflected and realized. I bless
it, if Israel does not regard emancipation as
the goal of its task, but only as a new condition of its mission, and as a new trial, much
severer than the trial of oppression ; but I
should grieve if Israel understood itself so
little, and had so little comprehension of its
own spirit that it would welcome emancipation
as the end of the Galuth, and the highest goal
of its historic mission. If Israel regards this
glorious concession merely as a means of
securing a greater degree of comfort in life,
and greater opportunities for the acquisition
of wealth and enjoyments, it would show that
Israel had not comprehended the spirit of its
own Law, nor learnt aught from the Galuth.
But sorrowfully, indeed, would I mourn, if
Israel should so far forget itself as to deem
emancipation—increased room for the acquisition of gain and pleasure through freedom
from unjust oppression—not too dearly pur-
chased through capricious curtailment of the

Torah, capricious abandonment of the chief element of our vitality. We must become Jews, Jews in the true sense of the word, permitting the spirit of the Law to pervade our entire being, accepting it as the fountain of life spiritual and ethical; then will Judaism gladly welcome emancipation as affording a greater opportunity for the fulfillment of its task, the realization of a noble and ideal life.

SEVENTEENTH LETTER.

You are right. The whole question of emancipation, which only concerns our external state, possesses but a subordinate interest for Judaism. Sooner or later the nations will decide what attitude they should take in the issue between right and wrong, between humanity or inhumanity, and the first awakening of a nobler sentiment than the mere lust for possession and enjoyment, the first expression of a livelier appreciation of the universal Lordship and Fatherhood of God, and of the earth as a Holy Land, given by Him to all men for the fulfillment of mankind's task, will speedily take effect in the emancipation of all the oppressed, and, therefore, also in that of the Jews.

Emancipation, like our external state altogether, is a matter, religiously speaking, of secondary consideration. We may, indeed, take part in accelerating its coming, but in itself it makes us neither greater nor smaller.

There is another goal before us, whose attainment depends entirely upon our own
efforts; it is the refinement and ennoblement of
ourselves, the fulfillment of Judaism by Jews.

This leads to a consideration of the topic
which you designate by the term " Reform."

Certainly, dear Benjamin, we are far from
being what we should be, and if you compare
the life ideal, which the Torah desires us to
realize, even according to the scanty outlines
which I have drawn for you in these letters,
with our actual life as individuals and as a
community, you will at once discern how
numerous are the steps which we must still
make, and how great the distance yet to be
climbed before we can reach the glorious summit of our aspiration and our hope.   Therefore, may our motto be—Reform ; let us strive
with all our power, with all the good and
noble qualities of our character to reach this
height of ideal perfection—Reform.

Its only object, however, must be the fulfillment of Judaism by Jews in our time, fulfillment of the eternal idea in harmony with the

conditions of the time; education, progress to
the Torah height, not, however, lowering the
Torah to the level of the age, cutting down
the towering summit to the sunken grade of
our life. We Jews need to be reformed
through Judaism, newly comprehended by the
spirit and fulfilled with the utmost energy; but
merely to seek greater ease and comfort in life
through the destruction of the eternal code set
up for all ages by the God of Eternity, is not
and never can be Reform. Judaism seeks to
lift us up to its height, how dare we attempt
to drag it down to our level?

Undoubtedly you recognize the evil defect
of our time; ignorance or false views of
Judaism, combined with a tendency, penetrat-
ing from the outer world into our humble
habitations, to look upon enjoyment as the
chief aim of life.

Alas! how widespread is ignorance, how
rare the Jew who knows himself, his purpose
in life, and the meaning of his history! Where
are the sons of Israel in whose breast echo the
tones of the harp of David and the words of

the prophets, and whose mind—but, ah! I should be silent concerning the mind—comprehends the extent of the Israel-duty? And what wrong and mischievous notions exist concerning the principles, ordinances, and teachings of Judaism? Even that which is known externally and superficially, how little is it known as regards its wondrously profound inner meaning! For instance, the Edoth duties, so useful and indispensable through the lessons they teach, are looked upon by some as mere mechanical *opus operatum*, or as talismanic jugglery for the prevention of physical evils or the erection of mystic supramundane worlds. Others again look upon the holiest laws of righteousness as matters outside of Judaism, not, as they should regard them, indissolubly interwoven with its very fabric.

As for those highly important laws of Judaism, which strengthen us to do battle with the sensual lusts of appetite and passion, of indulgence and ease, how little are they understood, how often denounced as cruel privation

beyond the power of human nature to endure;
how can they otherwise than succumb in this
unequal combat, since their victory is gained
by the spirit, and that is either absent or
wofully deficient? This inner conception is
lacking, comprehension of Judaism, of the
significance of its historic mission and teachings, and, therefore, love for it has no soil
upon which to grow. How extreme the re-
sultant danger is can be conceived when we
consider that this love is our only counter-
balance against internal and external temptation, and the attainment of this love our aim
and our only salvation. Compare with this
view the tendencies of contemporary Reform.
Be wroth with none, respect all, for they all
feel the shortcomings which exist, all wish that
which is good, as they conceive it; all desire
sincerely the welfare of Israel, and if they have
failed to recognize the good and have erred in
their comprehension of the truth, not they are
chiefly to blame; the entire past bears the res-
ponsibility together with them. You should,
therefore, respect their intentions, but you

may well mourn and weep when you examine
the aims to which their efforts are directed.
Is that the Reform we need, to take a standpoint outside of Judaism, to accept a conception derived from strangers, of the purposes of
human life, and the object of liberty, and
then, in correspondence with this borrowed
notion, to cut, curtail, and obliterate the
tenets and ordinances of Judaism? Is that
the Reform we desire, to remain within Judaism, uncomprehended Judaism, and to confine one's effort to modifying the external
form of an uncomprehended part of Judaism,
the service, in accordance with the demands of
an age, abounding in hollow sentimentality,
but sadly deficient in sound reflection and
thought, substituting for things misunderstood and abolished other things equally uncomprehended; nothing instituted or originated
to emphasize or perpetuate any true inner
sentiment of our faith? And as for the religious education of the young, which should
be the bearer of all our hopes for the future,
how is it situated?

Education, indeed, is not lacking; our youth are made thoroughly capable of contending vigorously in the struggle for bread ; handi-work, commerce, art, science—all these are carefully inculcated and the mind developed, although even in this regard more attention is paid to the mere strengthening of the memory than to the cultivation of habits of thought ; but the culture of the heart, the inculcation of Judaism, its emphatic presentation by the school resulting in its consequent infiltration through life, the rearing of human beings who will comprehend themselves as beings living in a Divine world and endowed with Divine powers, which they shall dedicate to the fulfillment of the Divine will ; human beings who shall rejoice in their mission and be filled with fiery love for the name " Jew," which summons them to such a life, to fulfill the Divine law amidst perils, sufferings, and privations ; human beings who comprehend the world, the past and the present and them-selves as corner-stones in the edifice of the future—if we seek such, we find a vacuum.

Take one of the religious books in your
hand and what will you find, a life-principle
drawn from outside of Judaism, the thirteen
creeds upon which Judaism perhaps stands,
but of which it is not composed, and a few
moral principles deduced from the Ten Commandments, the Chukkim and Edoth not
mentioned, or but slightly, as the so-called
ceremonial law in the appendix. It is all
more or less the reflection of catechisms, originated upon a different domain, for totally
different purposes. Among those, again, who
do not use these catechisms we find taught the
merest word-knowledge of the Torah, sometimes not even that; and as for the duties,
they are merely taught for practice, in the
most superficial manner, but without the
slightest elucidation or spiritual fervor, to
insure their comprehension and retention in
life. Whence, in Heaven's name, shall Jews
come, Jews inspired with the living spirit of
the knowledge of God and their mission, and
girded with strength to do battle against sensuality and error, against the troubles and

sorrows of time? You see—but why continue the gloomy picture? Let us rejoice that at least Israel's youth is not inferior to others in intellect and morality, even. though far removed from the ideals of Judaism. Let us rejoice at the activity within Judaism, even though much of it is but destruction or the painting over of rotten parts. This is the pledge of a better time. Let us try to outline the methods for obtaining a desirable reconstruction and a reform which appears to us true.

EIGHTEENTH LETTER.

The very essence of Israel's being rests upon the Torah; in it is our basis and our goal, from it the vital fluid in our veins. If our relation to it, the law of life and truth, be healthy and normal, Israel can suffer no ill; if sick, Israel cannot be well. There is no evil, no wrongful development in Judaism which does not owe its origin to an improper or sinful comprehension of the Torah, or at least is perpetuated thereby. Our sages with profound insight point to this as the true cause of the first national downfall, שלא ברכו בתורה תחלה, that they did not study the Law with the firm resolve to fulfill it in life and for life; life, the practical daily life of the world, fled from the Law, and the Law could not therefore properly pervade life, could not adequately enlighten it and inspire it with its, the Law's, own genial warmth.

If you search for the cause of our modern

sickness, you will find it nowhere else than in this fatal misconception and misapprehension. Originally only the fundamental teachings of Israel's Law were fixed in written form, the so-called written Law, ‏תי״ש״ב״כ‏, but the broader application thereof, in particular the spirit, which is the life, was to be preserved only in the living word, the so-called oral law, ‏תי״ש״ב״פ‏. The oppressions and afflictions of the times and the dispersion of Israel threatened destruction to the traditional science; the great and holy men who stood at the nation's head, yielding to necessity, decreed that the Mishnah be written down as far as its mere external word was conceived, but its spirit was still left to the traditional exposition of the living word. Increased external sorrows demanded more; they put into writing the spirit of the Mishnah in the Gemara, but the spirit of the Gemara was still reserved for oral interpretation. The affliction increased, making further safeguards necessary; they put the spirit of Bible and Gemara into the Aggadoth or allegorical in-

terpretations, but disguised and veiled so tnat
personal research should still be required to
discover the true spirit of the traditional
teachings thus perpetuated.

In two academies[1] the Law and the spirit
sought refuge, but passion and error soon
sapped the foundations of these noble institutions and destroyed them; the Law went into
exile, the letter and its external practical fulfillment were saved, but the spirit, preserved
only in the symbolical concealment of the letter, disappeared. The spirit could only be
comprehended by deduction from the letter
and the veiling symbol, together with the
higher insight which individuals had preserved. In that dark time there were not
lacking individuals who shone forth conspicuous through the true understanding of the
spirit of Judaism which they possessed, but
they were the exceptions; not all were endowed
with such mental elevation.

Israel's youth, as a rule, trained their minds
in non-Jewish schools, in independent, philo-

---

[1] Sura and Pumbaditha.

sophic studies, and drew from Arabic sources
the concepts of the Greek philosophy. As
the highest purpose of human existence they
learned to consider self-perfectation through
the knowledge of truth. Their awakened
minds felt themselves in contradiction to Judaism, whose spirit they did not comprehend;
their life-view was opposed to a view of life
which lays chiefest stress upon the deed, upon
action, and looks upon knowledge only as a
means to such action. The age gave birth to
a man,[1] a mind, who, the product of uncomprehended Judaism and Arabic science, was
obliged to reconcile the strife which raged in
his own breast in his own manner, and who,
by proclaiming it to the world, became the
guide of all in whom the same conflict existed.

This great man, to whom, and to whom
alone, we owe the preservation of practical
Judaism to our time, is responsible, because he
sought to reconcile Judaism with the difficulties which confronted it from without, instead
of developing it creatively from within, for all

---

[1] Maimonides.

the good and the evil which bless and afflict
the heritage of the father.   His peculiar mental tendency was Arabic-Greek, and his conception of the purpose of life the same.   He
entered into Judaism from without, bringing
with him opinions of whose truth he had convinced himself from extraneous sources and—
he reconciled.   For him, too, self-perfecting
through the knowledge of truth was the highest aim, the practical he deemed subordinate.
For him knowledge of God was the end, not
the means; hence he devoted his intellectual
powers to speculations upon the essence of
Deity, and sought to bind Judaism to the
results of his speculative investigations as to
postulates of science or faith.   The Mizvoth
became for him merely ladders, necessary only
to conduct to knowledge or to protect against
error, this latter often only the temporary and
limited error of polytheism.   Mishpatim became only rules of prudence, Mitzvoth as
well; Chukkim rules of health, teaching right
feeling, defending against the transitory errors
of the time ; Edoth ordinances, designed to

promote philosophical or other concepts; all
this having no foundation in the eternal essence
of things, not resulting from their eternal
demand on me, or from my eternal purpose
and task, no eternal symbolizing of an unchangeable idea, and not inclusive enough to
form a basis for the totality of the commandments.

He, the great systematic orderer of the practical results of the Talmud, gives expression
in the last part of his philosophic work to
opinions concerning the meaning and purpose
of the commandments which, taking the very
practical results codified by himself as the contents of the commandments, are utterly untenable—cast no real light upon them, and cannot
go hand in hand with them in practice, in life,
and in science. These are the views which
have been inherited up to the present day by
those who care at all to understand the spirit
of the Mitzvoth. But since the precepts, as
practically fulfilled, stand entirely out of connection with these explanations, it was inevitable that their ceremonial fulfillment lost its

spiritual basis, and became despised. You
see, instead of taking one's stand within Judaism, and asking, "Inasmuch as Judaism makes
these demands of me, what opinion of the purpose of man must it have?" instead of comprehending each demand in its totality according to
Bible and Talmud, and then asking, "What is
the reason and idea of this injunction?" people set up their standpoints outside of Judaism,
and sought to draw it over to them; they conceived *a priori* opinions as to what the Mitzvoth might be, without disturbing themselves
as to the real appearance of the Mitzvoth in all
its parts. What was the consequence? After
these opinions had brought about the natural
phenomenon that men who believed themselves the possessors of the knowledge which
the commandments were designed to inculcate, thought themselves absolved both from
the fulfillment of the commandment, intended
only as a guide, and from the study of the
science of the commandments, which had lost
for them all intellectual significance; other
men, possessed of a deeper comprehension of

Judaism, became at first enemies of this philosophical spirit, and later, of all specifically intellectual and philosophical pursuits in general.
Certain misunderstood utterances[1] were taken
as weapons with which to repel all higher
intellectual interpretation of the Talmud;
no distinction was made between the question, "What is stated here?" and the question, "Why is it stated?" and not even the
category of Edoth, which, according to its
whole nature, was designed to stir the mind
to activity, was excluded from the excommu-
nication of the intellectual. Another misunderstood passage, (ד״ה ״תוס א כ״ד סנהדרין
בלולה), even led later to the suppression of
Bible study, an error against which Proph-
ecy expressly warns (ו ט פ סופרים מס׳
ה״ל״ט). The inevitable consequence was,
therefore, that since oppression and persecu-

[1] For instance, ט״י, א״מ כ״ת, מ״ד, לד לד ב״ר. The injunction not to קרא דרשינן טעמא, which was often held up to me,
has no other than the very proper meaning that we should not
attach any importance in practical decision to the conjectural
reason of a Mitzvah, because it is only conjecture.

See also רמ״בן to the Torah ט״י, ט״י קדושים.

tion had robbed Israel of every broad and
natural view of the world and of life, and the
Talmud had yielded about all the practical
results for life of which it was capable, every
mind that felt the desire of independent activity was obliged to forsake the paths of
study and research in general open to the
human intellect, and to take its recourse to
dialectic subtleties and hair-splittings. Only
a very few during this entire period stood
with their intellectual efforts entirely within
Judaism, and built it up out of its own
inner concepts. Most distinguished among
them are the author of the "Cuzari," and
the son of Nachman. This condition of uncomprehended Judaism became particularly
prevalent in Germany, where ages of persecu-
tion and oppression suppressed every freer
upward movement of the mind. The general
fundamental principle, God the All-One and
the Torah His will, and the fulfillment of the
Law in the fear of God and with love for, and
faith in Him, retained, however, everywhere
its living force; and life, with all its posses-

sions and all its pleasures, was offered with magnificent devotion as a willing sacrifice to it.   A form of learning came into existence, concerning which, as a layman, I do not venture to express a judgment, but which, if I comprehend aright the little that I know, is an invaluable repository of the spirit of Bible and Talmud, but which has been, unfortunately, misunderstood; and what should have been eternal, progressive development, was considered a stationary mechanism, and the inner significance and concept thereof as extramundane dream-worlds.   This learning came into existence, and the mind turned either to the external ingenious development of the Talmud, or to this learning, which appealed to the emotions as well.   Practical Judaism, which, comprehended in its purity, would perhaps have been impregnated with the spiritual became in it, through misconception, a magical mechanism, a means of influencing or resisting theosophic worlds and anti-worlds.

Little by little there came into the hands of the people a part of a work, originally intended

only as a compendium for the learned and
containing the last results of Talmudic legal
science, codified for ceremonial practice.   It
was essentially nothing but a differently arranged edition of the systematic work of
Maimonides, by which this latter had become
the great preserver of practical Judaism in the
times of the greatest Galuth-oppression.   Unfortunately, however, it was almost exclusively
one part of this work which came into the
hands of people, containing only the divisions
Edoth and Abodah, referring to worship and
holy days; the other parts, which treat of the
other duties, were left for the learned, and did
not become the possession of the people.
Gradually the unfortunate opinion developed
that Judaism meant nothing but praying and
keeping holy days; its significance for life in
general remained unrecognized.

Considering all these influences together,
you will be able to comprehend the appearance
which Judaism presented, say, eighty years
ago.   The subsequent events will also be
intelligible to you.   When the external yoke

began to grow lighter, and the spirit felt itself freer, then arose a brilliant, respect-inspiring personality, Mendelssohn, which by its commanding influence has led the later development up to this day. This commanding individual, who had not drawn his mental development from Judaism, who was great chiefly in philosophical disciplines, in metaphysics, and æsthetics, who treated the Bible only philologically and æsthetically, and did not build up Judaism as a science from itself, but merely defended it against political stupidity and pietistic Christian audacity, and who was personally an observant Jew, accomplished this much, that he showed the world and his brethren that it was possible to be a strictly religious Jew and yet to shine distinguished as the German Plato. [1]

---

[1] Do not misunderstand me. I speak here only of the total impression of his work for Judaism. His "Jerusalem," which defends, on Jewish grounds, liberty of thought and faith, emphasizes also, in contradistinction to the Moreh, the practical essence of Judaism, and gives utterance to an opinion concerning the Edoth, which, had it been carried out and intellectually comprehended by his successors, might have revolutionized the subsequent period. But neither the one thing nor the other

This " and yet " was decisive. His followers contented themselves with developing Bible
study in the philologic-æsthetic sense, with
studying the Moreh, and with pursuing and
spreading humanistic letters ; but Judaism,
Bible and Talmud as Jewish science, were neglected. Even the most zealous study of the
Bible was of no avail for the comprehension
of Judaism, because it was not treated as the
authoritative source of doctrine and instruction, but only as a beautiful poetic storehouse
from which to draw rich supplies for the fancy
and the imagination. The Talmud thus neglected, practical Judaism thus completely uncomprehended, it was but natural that the former symbolizing and abstract interpretation of
Judaism, which had for a time been inter-
rupted, again became prevalent, and was
carried to an extreme which threatened to

---

took place. The science of Judaism was not further developed
by him, and his successors, lacking the religious sentiment of
the Master, did not rest content under the idea of the eternally
binding power of Divine revelation, and could do nothing better for the intellectual comprehension of the Law, than to surrender completely to the Maimonidean theories.

destroy all Judaism. If that view of life be
true, which places the highest mission of man
n the recognition of truth; and who could
venture to doubt it, seeing that Maimonides
has declared so; above all, if those views concerning the requirements of the Torah be true;
and who could dare to think otherwise, since
Maimonides, the great authority on Talmud,
and himself an observant Jew, had propounded
them; then, indeed, the many-foliod Talmud
is nothing but a wearisome mass of hair-splitting subtleties, useful only for the accumulation of dust and moths; then, indeed, is practical Judaism nothing but unreasoning weari-
ness of the flesh: who could resist this conclusion ?

If, for instance, the sole purpose of the
prohibition of labor on the Sabbath was to
enable men to rest and recover from the toils
of the week, if the Sabbath means only the
cessation of corporeal activity in order that
the mind may be active; and who could doubt
it, since both Moses interpret it thus, and the
Christian Sunday agrees with their conception,

who must not consider it mere pettiness and pedantic absurdity to fill an entire folio with the investigation of the question, what particular actions are forbidden, and what permitted on the Sabbath day? How singular, to declare the writing of two letters, perhaps an intellectual occupation, a deadly sin, while judging leniently many acts involving great physical exertion, and freeing from penalty all purposeless destruction! Why, it even forbids the hen to lay eggs! Or, to go over to another domain, if sacrifice means only to give of one's possessions in grateful recognition that they come from God, or if, in its special Biblical form, it was mainly designed as a protest against the polytheistic sacrificial usages then prevailing; how absurd it is, to fill three or four folios with investigations concerning the manner of offering sacrifice, the part which might be used, the persons who might officiate, and the permissible times! Do you not see, that all this is only mind-destroying priest-craft? Therefore; therefore—many conclusions could be and were drawn, but before drawing them, people should have asked themselves, "Is Moses the son of Maimon, or Moses the son of Mendel, really identical with Moses the son of Amram?" Is there not contained in this dissonance between the theory of the Mitzvah and its reality a proof that the explanation is not right, that it is not based upon the complete conception of the Mitzvah, but is—dreamed into it from without?

Does not the Moreh itself say that in forming the concept of the Mitzvoth it uses the written Law only as the basis, a standpoint which Maimonides himself would have declared incorrect for the practical fulfillment, and which cannot, therefore, be considered aught else than irrational?

Does he not himself say that in considering the significance of the Mitzvoth he has overlooked those details which, in their totality, give the complete idea of the Mitzvoth, and which form the main subjects of discussion in the Oral Law? (Moreh Nebuchim, Chapters XXVI and XLI.) There must be sense in all the commandments, in particular as regards

those which announce themselves as instructive, which call themselves Testimony, Memorial, Symbol. It must be possible to find the
indwelling spirit of these; how would it be to
try to do so, to make once ,the experiment?
This attempt has hitherto never been made.
Many did not wish to make the attempt nor to
attain to the result. A spirit had come from the
West, which mocked at everything holy, and
knew no greater pleasure than to make them
ridiculous, and together with it there entered
a longing for sensual enjoyments, which
eagerly embraced the opportunity to rid itself
so easily of burdensome restrictions. These
motives combined to induce people to tear
down the barriers erected by the Law, until
human conduct became one dead, dull level.[1]

---

[1] A word here concerning the true method of Torah-investiga-
tion. Two revelations are open before us, nature—and Torah.
In nature all phenomena stand before us as indisputable facts,
and we can only endeavor *a posteriori* to ascertain the law of
each and the connection of all. Abstract demonstration of the
truth or, rather, the probability of theoretic explanations of
the facts of nature, is an unnatural proceeding. The right
method is to verify our assumptions by the known facts, and
the highest attainable degree of certainty is to say, " The facts

And what is our present state? The first delights of the worldly spirit have passed away, other generations have succeeded to

agree with our assumption "—that is, all observed phenomena can be explained according to our theory. A singly contradictory phenomenon will make our theory untenable. We must, therefore, acquire all possible knowledge concerning the object of our investigation, and know it, if possible, in its totality. If, however, all efforts should fail in disclosing the inner law and connection of phenomena revealed to us as facts in nature, the facts remain, nevertheless, undeniable, and cannot be reasoned away. The same principles must be applied to the investigation of the Torah. In the Torah, as in nature, God is the ultimate cause; in the Torah, as in nature, no fact may be denied, even though the reason and the connection may not be comprehended; as in nature, so in the Torah, the traces of Divine wisdom must ever be sought for. Its ordinances must be accepted in their entirety as undeniable phenomena, and must be studied in accordance to their connection with each other, and the subject to which they relate. Our conjectures must be tested by their precepts, and our highest certainty here also can only be that everything stands in harmony with our theory. But as in nature, the phenomena are recognized as facts, though their cause and relation to each other may not be understood, and are independent of our investigation, but rather the contrary is the case; in the same way the ordinances of the Torah must be law for us, even if we do not comprehend the reason and the purpose of a single one. Our fulfillment of the commandments must not depend upon our investigations. Only the commandments belonging to the category Edoth, which are designed to impress the intellectual and emotional life, are incomplete without such research.

those who witnessed the first change in Jewish
sentiment, and to-day two diametrically oppo-
site parties confront each other. The one
party has inherited uncomprehended Judaism
as a mechanical habit, מצות אנשים מלומדה,
without its spirit; they bear it in their hands
as a sacred relic, a revered mummy, and fear
to rouse its spirit. The others are partly filled
with noble enthusiasm for the welfare of the
Jews, but look upon Judaism as a lifeless
framework, as something which should be laid
in the grave of a long since dead and buried
past. They seek its spirit and find it not, and
are in danger, with all their efforts to help the
Jew, of severing the last life-nerve of Judaism
—ignorantly. And to-day, when, despite a
thousand shades and variations of difference,
these two opposing elements agree in the one
great circumstance, that they are both wrong
—what shall be done? What is the way to
salvation? Does it suffice for the salvation of
Judaism to establish our schools upon such a
two-fold basis, and to reform our form of worship? The spirit, the inner harmonious life-

principle, is lacking, and that you cannot supply through polishing the outside frame.

There is one way to salvation;—where the sin was committed the atonement must begin, —and this one way is, to forget the inherited prejudices and opinions concerning Judaism; to go back to the sources of Judaism, to Bible, Talmud, and Midrash; to read, study, and comprehend them in order to live them; to draw from them the teachings of Judaism concerning God, the world, mankind, and Israel, according to history and precept; to know Judaism out of itself; to learn from its own utterances its science of life. With the Bible the beginning should be made, its language should first be comprehended, and then out of the spirit of the speech the spirit of the speakers should be inferred. The Bible should not be studied as an interesting object of philological or antiquarian research, not as basis for theories of taste or for amusement; it should be studied as the foundation of a new science; with Davidic sentiment nature should be contemplated; with the ear of an Isaiah history

should be listened to, and then, with eye thus
aroused, with ear thus opened, the doctrine of
God, world, man, Israel, and Torah should be
drawn from the Bible, and should become an
idea, or system of ideas, fully comprehended.
In this spirit Talmud should be studied, in the
Halachah only further elucidation and amplifi-
cation of ideas already known from the Bible
should be sought for; in the Aggadah only
figuratively disguised manifestation of the
same spirit. This path you should pursue,
unconcerned as to the opinion which the one
or the other school of misled ones may hold in
reference to your methods of study; unconcerned that your simplicity of interpretation
will not permit you to shine among the heroes
of hair-splitting, life-ignoring disputations;
unconcerned if you do not shine in the special
disciplines which you use only as auxiliary
sciences for your general object; unconcerned
if you are no longer qualified for pretentious
appearance. All this should concern you little, for you are learning what is better, to
know the light, the truth, the warmth, and

the sublimity of life, and when you have attained to this you will comprehend Israel's history and Israel's Law, and that life, in its true sense, is the reflection of that Law, permeated with that spirit. One spirit lives in all, from the construction of the Holy Tongue to the construction of the universe and the plan of life, one spirit, the spirit of the All-One! That would be a task for the disciples of science! But the results of that science must be carried over into life, transplanted by schools. Schools for Jews! The young saplings of your people should be reared as Jews, trained to become sons and daughters of Judaism, as you have recognized and comprehended and learned to respect and love it as the law of your life. The language of the Bible and the language of the land should be theirs; in both they should be taught to think; their heart should be taught to feel, their mind to think; the Scriptures should be their book of law for life, and they should be able to comprehend life through their word.

Their eye should be open to recognize the

world around them as God's world and themselves in God's world as His servants; their
ear should be open to perceive in history the
narrative of the education of *all* men to this
service. The wise precepts of Torah and
Talmud should be made clear to them as
designed to spiritualize their lives for such
sublime service of God, and they should be
taught to comprehend, respect, and love them,
in order that they might rejoice in the name
"Jew" despite all which that name implies
of scorn and privation. Together with this
instruction they should be fitted for bread-
winning, but they should be taught that bread-
winning is only a means, not the purpose of
life, and that the value of life is not to be
judged according to rank, wealth, or splendor,
but according to the amount of good and of
service to God with which it is filled. They
should be taught not to subordinate the
demands of their spiritual mission to those of
sensuality and comfort, but the reverse, and
while this training was going on, and until
Israel's houses were built up of such sons and

daughters, the parents should be implored and entreated not to destroy the work of the school, not to crush or choke with icy and unsympathetic mood the tender shoots of Jewish sentiment in the breasts of their children. The latent germs of a nobler disposition in the breast of parents should also be stirred, and if this be impossible, at least they should be forced to respect the sentiments they could not comprehend nor share. If these ends should be earnestly striven for, it would be different in Israel.

It will be different in Israel; our time leads necessarily to such a change. Do not think our time so dark and hopeless, friend; it is only nervous and uncertain, as a woman in childbirth. But better the anxiety which prevails in the house of a woman about to give birth, than the freedom from anxiety, but also from joy and hope, in the house of the barren one. This time of labor may outlast our lives and the lives of our children and grandchildren, but our later posterity will rejoice in the child that has struggled out into light and life, and its name will be "self-comprehending Judaism."

The age offers one pledge for the accomplishment of this result; it is the effort to think, to comprehend and to grasp with the mind that which should be respected and revered. Truly, when the mind will have realized the futility of this baseless and aimless striving, of its bargaining with the overestimated demands of the fleeting moment; when it will have clearly brought to its consciousness that the noble life can only be erected upon ideas inwardly recognized as true, then will arise the question, "What does it mean that I am a Jew? What is Judaism?" Nor will the answer to this question be sought at the cathedras or in the writings of non-Jewish scholars, who often see Judaism through a distorting glass and who sometimes think it necessary to destroy the teachings of Torah and Judaism in order to establish their own notions. Neither will it be sought in the writings of time-serving reformers influenced by external motives, nor in the writings of

Jewish scholars who take their standpoint outside of Judaism. But the seekers after knowledge will go back to the ancient fountains of
Judaism, Bible and Talmud, and the one effort
will be to obtain the concept of life out of Judaism and to comprehend Judaism as the law of
life, and this effort will lead to the transposing
of that which holds the theory of truth and life
into actual, practical truth and life, in accordance with the old adage, now, alas, nearly
forgotten, ללמוד וללמד לשמור ולעשות,
"to learn and to teach, to keep and to do."

O, that you all, who mean well with Judaism, which you have inherited as a habit, and
which you are thinking of handing down as a
habit, O, that your eyes might be opened and
that you might recognize that only through
the spirit can you hand it down ; O, that you
might at least hand to your sons and daughters
the Holy Writings, the writings of the Torah,
the Prophets, and the Hagiographa, so that
the spirit which throbs in them might become
their light and support in life ; O, that you
noble-minded ones, who think that you labor

for the weal of Judaism; O, that you might
consider that when you strike the chains from
hand and foot or don fine clothing and adorn
your outward persons, you do not yet help to
improve or elevate life. Lower again the
hand upraised to strike down the battlements of
your faith, and consider whether you are not
about to destroy an edifice which, even though
in its covering of the dust of centuries, it appears to you worthy only of the axe's stroke,
may yet contain things holy and eternal, things
of life and truth; turn again toward it your
averted gaze and examine what it is from which
you turn away.   Is it the fault of the object
—should the object be held blameworthy, if
those who represent it, themselves covered with
the dust of the battlefield upon which they
struggle against oppression and misery, could
only rescue it dust-covered and made repulsive?
Should we, to whom the mildness of the times
has given the task of rubbing off the dust,
think so little of the troubles and battles of
those men as not even to deem it worth while
to dust off the jewel for our own benefit, but,

regarding only the dust-covered exterior, cast away as worthless the precious possession for which our ancestors sacrificed life, and property, and liberty, and all the joys of life? Should—but I forget, my dear Benjamin, that only heaven hears these wishes, that only this paper sees them, and that only to you will they be shown; I forget that I am writing only to you. Light and truth and life will emerge from this time of trial; be sure of that, friend, and then you will regard differently that which I was accustomed to lament with you, the apparently chaotic condition of the spiritual affairs of our people; no government, no authority, all efforts solely individual, and, through the lust for reform, the religious service, about which the whole movement turns, has become so variegated that a Jew, travelling through Germany, might almost find it different in every congregation. Do you not see that this also may have its good? I am convinced that none of those of us now living comprehend Judaism in its true purity and truth. Consider also the divergency of

opinions, quite natural inasmuch as almost
every Rabbi strikes out his own path and is
led by no schools. Consider furthermore that
we are only in the time of labor; it would be
unfortunate if an authority tried to establish
something—it would only make our sorrows
eternal! It would be impossible to select
proper men. If one-sided, they would perpetuate extravagances; if composed of mingled
elements representing various ideas, their creation would be a half-thing, a torso, and would
only serve to dam the stream of development,
which can only bring pure and living water
when permitted to flow to its uttermost end.
Time, if left unhindered, will wash away what
it itself has brought into existence, and room
will always remain for the higher edifice which
yet awaits us. I think that if, in the period
after Maimonides, anxiety for the maintenance
of Judaism in external practice had not made
it necessary to suppress antagonistic efforts,
centuries ago the improper tendencies of the
Jewish spirit would, through the very completeness of their fulfillment, have brought

about sober reflection upon the nature and purposes of our faith, and we would now be whither we can only expect to come in centuries. Under present conditions I rejoice that the scales hang free, held by God alone, and that only intellectual efforts mutually balance each other, but that no temporal power can interpose the sword to check the freedom of the swinging. If it should be stopped, our great grandchildren would be no better off than we. Should we fear to go through the period of anxiety for them?

Let the scales swing! The freer they hang, and the more violently now they swing up and down, the truer and purer will be the estimate of the right principle of faith and life which they will finally fix. And whèn the scales have ceased to swing, and when all luminous will stand in Israel, the Spirit of Understanding, רוח בינה, the spirit which understands itself, its history, and its law, when its throbbing impulse of life will have pervaded all its members; when the branch gone forth from Israel shall have performed its mission and fought to victory a battle of another kind in the midst of our non-Jewish brethren; when the free gaze uplifted to the All-One, and the consciousness of inner moral power shall have conquered whatever dims the eye and corrupts noble vigor . . . then will the book of our history have been written, and its final teachings will have penetrated all spirits. Let us comprehend our time, dear Benjamin, and let every one, according to the measure of intellectual and spiritual power vouchsafed him, strive to further the progress to the goal, each in the greater or smaller circle in which he lives. Thousands may forsake the cause of life and light, thousands may tear themselves away from the lot and the name of Israel, whose mode of life they have long since rejected—the cause of truth counts not the number of its adherents. If only one remains —one Jew with the book of the law in his hand, with Israel's law in his heart, Israel's light in his spirit—that one suffices; Israel's cause is not lost. When Israel had grown unfit for its mission, the All-One desired to

permit the law and the mission of Israel to be
borne by the one Moses, and the prophet tells
us timid ones the same truth:

"Gaze upon the rock from which we were
  hewn,
Upon the fountain-hollowing mallet with which
  ye were dug!
Gaze upon Abraham, your father,
Upon Sarah, destined to bear ye.
One only was he when I called him;
I blessed him and made him many."

Farewell, dear Benjamin, train yourself to
be such a one; farewell.

NINETEENTH LETTER.

You have prevailed, my Benjamin! On the
day when you consecrate unto yourself the
wife, with whose aid you are to erect a house
in Israel, I shall offer you the only present
you seek; I shall grant the request which you
have so often uttered to me. I shall, if God
gives me understanding and health, lay upon
my people's altar the only offering which, in
my weakness, I am able to place thereon. I
do not entertain in connection with it the san-
guine hopes with which you have welcomed
this resolve. I have revealed to you in writing and orally what I have cherished for a
long time as my dearest treasure, and you
have accepted it with warm appreciation as
truth; but I do not imagine on that account
that it will be acknowledged by all as truth,
or that I may deem it with certainty the pure
gold of truth. I know too well both my own
limitations and the character of the age to be

led astray by such roseate hopes. But I consider it the duty of every one, in a time of such solemn import, and in behalf of a cause which is to us the holiest and most sacred, to make known his opinions openly and honestly. And if I should only succeed in demonstrating that the matter has not been thoroughly investigated in all its aspects, that there is, perhaps, a way by means of which one could reach entirely different results than those hitherto attained, a view in the light of which everything would present an appearance quite different from that hitherto customary and usual; yes, if I should only succeed in staying one hand that had been too swiftly raised in order to tear down, and could induce its owner instead calmly to examine; indeed, if I could come no nearer to the goal that I have often pictured to you in letters than to induce another to step upon the road which I have prepared, another, more talented, more richly equipped with intellectual light and strength than I, and he should demonstrate so clearly the truth and dignity, the life and the light contained in the edifice of Judaism that my feeble attempts would arouse but a pitying smile and be forgotten; friend, my reward would even then be greater than I have dared to hope. Nor do you err when you think that modest diffidence has restrained me so long from undertaking a task which must long since have spoken within me.

That I have long since devoted my thoughts to this task, the accompanying roll of essays concerning Israel and Israel's duties—or rather concerning the duties alone, for my thoughts on Israel are still only a project of my mind— must convince you. But I have been, and still am, diffident, not on account of myself, but on account of the cause which I have ventured to represent.

In an age when the contrasts stand so sharply over against each other, and when truth is on neither side, in such an age the man who belongs to no party, who has only the cause in his heart, and serves it alone, cannot, unless he be a Divine master, who comprehends the Divine truth in its purity, and has the power to show it so brilliant in its Divine radiance that all spirits subdued acknowledge its divinity and do it homage, such a one cannot, I repeat, expect approval or agreement on any side.

This I knew and know, and with this knowledge within my mind I first took up the pen to these essays. Fame or acknowledgment of my personal merit are not the objects which I seek, or else they indeed would have been right whose judgment already sounds in my ears as that of the multitude: "He understands but ill the world and his time, and what it demands." No such motive has prompted me to these efforts, but only the inner voice which, though I listen and examine my inmost thoughts a thousand times, speaks ever to me the same words, saying: "There is some truth in your views, some of that truth which, you think, must ultimately struggle forth into the light of victory; the way upon which you have begun to walk is perhaps only a by-path, but it leads in the right direction, and if one abler than you should begin to pursue it, the cause of truth would surely prevail." This

voice alone stirred me on. Surely, friend, a
grain of truth is worth the sacrifice of my
person, even if I should sacrifice it a thousand
times. This care has never made me hesitate,
but other cares have filled me with anxiety,
when I asked myself whether I would not do
harm where I thought to help. The view of
the reconstruction of Judaism as a science I
have evolved almost alone out of my inner
consciousness. Only one dear friend assisted
me a little in the smaller, easier, and clearer
part, and only one star guided me somewhat
in the beginning. I have worked myself
through to the point where you found me.
But may it not be that upon this way, where
at every step thorns and refuse had to be
removed, and I, with my limited powers, was
called upon alone to take issue with the entire
past and the entire present, may it not well be,
I ask, that I have entered into a thousand
devious paths, and accepted a thousand errors
as truths? Is the edifice, as it stands within
me, and as I would show it to my brethren, is
it free from defects? And if the attempt

should fail, would not those who would like to erase from the book of life the cause for which I live, would they not make use of my unsuccessful attempts as a means of strangling the dearly beloved cause? How they would gloat over my failure and say, "See there, some new attempts to rehabilitate Judaism—entire failures!" I am not constituted for a writer; all my life I have thought more than spoken, spoken more than written; will I be able to write for truth with the clearness which convinces the mind, the power which captures the heart? I must, if I would speak to the children of the time, address them in German (*i. e.* modern) language and German writing, and as surely as I know that Judaism, rightly comprehended and rightly presented, unites all creatures with a band of love and justice, so surely do I also know that evil disposed calumniators can and do take isolated passages, torn out of their connection, interpreted in contradiction to their true spirit, and without consideration of the entire edifice of which they form but an insignificant part, and use

them as pointed arrows and ponderous cudgels
with which to smite and wound helpless vic-
tims. Will my efforts have a better fate? Will
not some one whose sensitive spirit has been
insulted and offended by rude audacity, be
able to point to me as the—even though inno-
cent—cause? Many other cares of a similar
kind oppressed me.

" How did you answer all these questions,"
I hear you ask, " since after all you did resolve
to undertake the work?" " Because," I
thought, " I have climbed alone to a height,
from which a new view displays itself to me.
On that very account it devolves on me to
summon companions, to descend and to begin
again the journey with the friends who will
join me. I only wish to give what I have
until now been able to gather together, not as
a perfect work, but truly ' as essays.' " Can
it injure the cause in the eyes of the sensible
if a single immature youth has, perhaps,
dreamed dreams that are utterly baseless and
unreal? Then there is the question of duty.
I see a child enveloped in flames; the bystand-

ers are timidly inactive, or seek only to save
the building.   I see the child,—I rush in;—
need I ask first my neighbor whether he, too,
sees the child; have I the right to consider
whether, in my hasty rush, I may not knock
some neighbor bloody; may I even ask whether,
in my haste to save the child, I am not hinder-
ing the task of saving the building or produ-
cing a draught, which may start the fire to
fresh activity? "But suppose you see the child
too late, and before you reach it the building
falls with hiss and crash upon its poor head?"

Even if it should bury me, too, in its ruins,
I would but have done my duty.

Of course, my dear Benjamin, the natural
way would have been to have labored first
only for the scientific evolvement, and whatever would have demonstrated in the battle of
minds its truth and tenability would have
been afterwards quietly transferred into the
practice of life.   That would have been the
quieter, the surer, the pleasanter way.

But our time demands a different course.
In Mendelssohn's days, when the new move-

ment of the spirit had begun but the Jewish
life was yet untouched, then it would have
been possible to construct the science of Judaism, and to bring to the strong formal life the
light and warmth of the spirit, and our condition would be different now.   To-day it is no
longer possible.   The opinions, not derived
from true Judaism, have become active and
vigorous, and labor with hostile energy to
undermine that which they pretend to represent.   They must be combatted directly in the
midst of life, so that many who still observe
may comprehend what they observe; that
many who reject may hesitate and examine
that which they reject; that many a hand,
now raised, perhaps, in honest zeal to tear
down or to build up something new, be held
back, and its owner be induced to inquire carefully concerning that which he had purposed
to tear down or to build in other form, and
with new additions.   Later it would devolve
upon the men of science to establish in science,
and as science, the principles which we had
actively defended in life.   That is the way in

which I intend to proceed. If Heaven will vouchsafe me health and understanding, I shall endeavor to declare in a first part the views on Judaism concerning God, the world, man, Israel, the Torah; in a second part to expound the Mitzvoth, as far as it is incumbent upon us, deprived of our national soil, to fulfill them; the passages of the Torah shall always precede; then shall follow the views concerning them with which the study of several years have furnished me, and then, for the purpose of practical fulfillment, extracts from the fourfold code, the Shulchan Aruch, shall follow. Everything shall be treated popularly, directly for life, and its demonstration in Jewish science shall be left as a later task, as you now have this part in your hands. I rejoice that the first impulse to these essays was derived from the necessity of supplying the teachers of the schools under my supervision with a book in which they could read themselves into Jews before they began to rear young souls for Judaism; and in elaborating them for larger circles of readers, I always thought of the intellectual youths and maidens of my people as their chief readers. This second part I intend—God willing—to publish first. To be sure you are right, in your description of the plan, that the knowledge of the general should precede that of the particular, and such is, indeed, the plan of my work. Nevertheless I shall publish the particular first. I know well that I will thereby rouse up more opponents, for people are readier to acknowledge principles before they have obtained a full view of the consequences to which they logically lead. Still I cannot do otherwise.

I recognize as our nearest and most fundamental evil the false opinions and notions which prevail concerning the extent as well as the contents and meaning of our Mitzvoth. In these isolated, uncomprehended tasks and duties Israel's essence is misunderstood, attacked, annihilated. At this spot the greatest stream flows away, and here the first effort should be made to repair the breach. When the demonstration has been given as to the special contents of Judaism, then the gaze may be lifted higher and the question be answered as to the position which Judaism, as a whole, occupies in the series of other phenomena, what its relation to mankind, what the position of man in the world as comprehended from Judaism, what the relation of the world to God, of God to it. If the first part appeared first, people would look upon that which I say of Israel as a mere dream picture, a creation of the enthusiastic fancy, nowhere existing in reality. In order, however, to give my readers as much knowledge of the general as is absolutely necessary to the understanding of the special, I shall first sketch out some general outlines, such as I tried to give you in the beginning of our correspondence, and I have endeavored in the case of each particular Mitzvah to lead the reader to an understanding of its significance as based upon its relation to Judaism in general.

So much, perhaps more than too much, for this project in which you take such warm interest. May you, if its results be not altogether without blessing, remember with joy that in a time when your eye could have been

turned with so many sweet hopes entirely
upon your own individual life, you had so
much love for the general and universal. May
the day on which you receive these lines be
for you the founder of a joyful, active future.
May the wife whom you to-day call "consecrated," be consecrated to you ever as your
holiest possession. May the house which you
establish together be pure and holy and godly,
as the holy symbol of the "robe"[1] with
which you enwrap yourselves. May the "cup
of life"[2] from which you both shall drink,
hold ever so much of the sweet that you shall
never despair, so much of the bitter that you
shall never grow over-proud; and may you accept all abundance of blessing as means given
you by the hand of God, to live a life of
righteousness and love. Farewell, my Benjamin, farewell. Your NAPHTALI.

THE END.

תם ונשלם שבח לאל בורא עולם

"It is finished and done. praised be God, Creator
of the world."

---

[1] The Tallith טלית. [2] The cup containing the wine of blessing

CPSIA information can be obtained at www.ICGtesting.com
Printed in the USA
LVOW082037260412

279310LV00001BA/198/P